STUDIES OF THE AMERICAS

edited by

Maxine Molyneux

Institute for the Study of the Americas
University of London
School of Advanced Study

Titles in this series are multidisciplinary studies of aspects of the societies of the hemisphere, particularly in the areas of politics, economics, history, anthropology, sociology, and the environment. The series covers a comparative perspective across the Americas, including Canada and the Caribbean as well as the United States and Latin America.

Titles in this series published by Palgrave Macmillan:

Cuba's Military 1990–2005: Revolutionary Soldiers during Counter-Revolutionary Times
By Hal Klepak

The Judicialization of Politics in Latin America
Edited by Rachel Sieder, Line Schjolden, and Alan Angell

Latin America: A New Interpretation
By Laurence Whitehead

Appropriation as Practice: Art and Identity in Argentina
By Arnd Schneider

America and Enlightenment Constitutionalism
Edited by Gary L. McDowell and Johnathan O'Neill

Vargas and Brazil: New Perspectives
Edited by Jens R. Hentschke

When Was Latin America Modern?
Edited by Nicola Miller and Stephen Hart

Debating Cuban Exceptionalism
Edited by Bert Hoffman and Laurence Whitehead

Caribbean Land and Development Revisited
Edited by Jean Besson and Janet Momsen

Cultures of the Lusophone Black Atlantic
Edited by Nancy Priscilla Naro, Roger Sansi-Roca, and David H. Treece

Democratization, Development, and Legality: Chile, 1831–1973
By Julio Faundez

The Hispanic World and American Intellectual Life, 1820–1880
By Iván Jaksić

The Role of Mexico's Plural *in Latin American Literary and Political Culture: From Tlatelolco to the "Philanthropic Ogre"*
By John King

Raúl Castro and Cuba

A Military Story

Hal Klepak

RAÚL CASTRO AND CUBA
Copyright © Hal Klepak, 2012.

All rights reserved.

First published in 2012 by
PALGRAVE MACMILLAN®
in the United States—a division of St. Martin's Press LLC,
175 Fifth Avenue, New York, NY 10010.

Where this book is distributed in the UK, Europe and the rest of the world,
this is by Palgrave Macmillan, a division of Macmillan Publishers Limited,
registered in England, company number 785998, of Houndmills,
Basingstoke, Hampshire RG21 6XS.

Palgrave Macmillan is the global academic imprint of the above companies
and has companies and representatives throughout the world.

Palgrave® and Macmillan® are registered trademarks in the United States,
the United Kingdom, Europe and other countries.

ISBN: 978–0–230–34074–9

Library of Congress Cataloging-in-Publication Data is available from the
Library of Congress.

A catalogue record of the book is available from the British Library.

Design by Newgen Imaging Systems (P) Ltd., Chennai, India.

First edition: July 2012

10 9 8 7 6 5 4 3 2 1

Printed in the United States of America.

*To Gordon and Linda Vachon, delightful friends to whom
I am thankful for so much over the years*

Contents

Avant Propos

An academic career spent largely on subjects of defense and armed forces is often seen by some who view themselves as more mainstream historians as somehow lost time. Many feel that these matters are somehow secondary or even uninteresting or, for some, even unworthy of interest for moral reasons. The sad fact remains, however, that military forces remain essential elements of most modern societies and that their actions in times of crisis are often decisive for the future of their nations. While this is unfortunate, it is nonetheless only too true. Nowhere is this more the case than in Latin America where the institution has known a dominant role in the post-independence politics of the region that cannot be denied. That very centrality, added to many other factors, has ensured that governments of almost all Latin American countries are often reticent to openly discuss their armed forces or the roles and history of those forces, not to speak of their present status, strength, and influence.

If this is true across the board, how much more so is it of the only Latin American country facing a simply massive defense task for over half a century, and where asymmetries of size and power are daunting in a way unknown in the rest of the hemisphere at any time in its history. Cuba has faced such a dramatic situation, with a massive and hostile nation—by far the most powerful in the world—only 150 kilometers away and determined to unseat its revolutionary experiment by almost any means and replace its political, economic, and social system with one more to that nation's liking.

In the huge undertaking to deter that nation from direct attack on the island, and to defeat its more informal and indirect attempts to destroy the Castro government, the Cuban armed and other security forces have had the central role for virtually all of that half-century. US opposition to Fidel taking power was visible (if diffuse through the Washington interagency battles) well before the revolutionary leader's triumph in January 1959. The new government's attempts

to settle into power were likewise hamstrung by elements in the
US embassy in any number of ways in the first days of that decisive
month after the military struggle to topple the Batista regime ended
with the taking of Havana by the flying columns of Che Guevara
and Camilo Cienfuegos, and of Santiago, Cuba's eastern "capital,"
by Fidel and Raúl Castro themselves in the first two days of the
new year.

As Fidel moved to implement an increasingly radical program that
could not fail to hurt totally dominant US economic interests on
the island, and especially with his application of a serious agrarian
reform program as of May of that first year, US opposition solidified
and began to take ever harsher forms. And even as this opposition
remained officially in the economic realm, the Eisenhower government approved both military and subversion programs that would
reinforce and complete those less visibly aggressive measures.

This story has continued in one form or another, sometimes
intense and sometimes less so, for over 50 years, and it has been the
constantly reformed armed and security forces of the island that have
borne the brunt of what all this has meant: assassination attempts on
Cuban leaders, what can only be termed terrorist attacks on Cuban
civilian targets, establishment and support of armed opposition
groups over many years on the island, organization and funding of
an invasion force for a direct military attack, structured planning for
attack with the regular forces of the United States, military maneu-
vers to intimidate the government in Havana, and espionage flights
over the island.

The answers to these threats were almost always in their essentials
the responsibility of the Cuban Armed Forces, the *Fuerzas, Armadas,
y Revolucionarias* (regulars, militias, and reserves), and their adjunct
comrades in arms in the *Policía Nacional Revolucionaria* (National
Revolutionary Police), the *Ministerio del Interior* (Ministry of the
Interior or MININT), and the other state security organs. These
institutions ad to build up the strength to deter direct attack from the
United States, defeat direct attack coming from that source but in the
guise of Cuban-Americans determined also to unseat Castro, root
out and destroy insurrectional and sabotage cadres usually inserted
into the island, attempt to deter and combat terror attacks on civilian targets, keep tabs on overflights, and directly protect the lives of
Cuban leaders, especially that of Fidel Castro himself.

It was largely in the hands of his younger brother Raúl Castro
that Fidel left the overall control of the construction of the state
apparatus that could manage all these tasks from the beginning of

his government. While Raúl only became formally minister of the Revolutionary Armed Forces in September of 1959 when the armed forces received their first major reforms of the revolutionary period, in reality he was in charge of them, of course under the very watchful eye of Fidel as *comandante en jefe* (commander in chief), from very early on indeed in the new government. And while more study is needed to know exactly the roles of the different senior officers of the army during the evolution of the situation in those first months, what is clear is that early on the nature of the threat meant that Raúl was the obvious choice for command of what was to be the Cuban defense system and the armed forces that were to be its bulwark.

He took the ragtag army of the Sierra Maestra insurrection, in the eastern mountains of the country, combined it with highly limited elements of the still dangerous regular army of the Batista era, and built the militias to make this army truly national and sufficiently large to contemplate real deterrence of a superpower. With Fidel he designed and implemented the novel strategies to make such deterrence a reality, and repeatedly handed his brother the instruments needed to undertake successfully all the tasks mentioned. This massive achievement is far too rarely seen for its true worth.

It is not easy to make a mark as the younger brother of a man who is deemed by most Latin American leaders of today to be the most influential man that region has produced since the legendary liberator Simón Bolívar, the man who freed Bolivia, Colombia, Ecuador, what is now Panama, and Venezuela in the epic struggles of 1810 through 1826. Fidel has such acknowledged charismatic, leadership, statesmanship, organizational, inspirational, oratorical, and other qualities, acknowledged even by many of his most ferocious opponents, that it would not be easy for anyone to be greatly noticed just below him in the national hierarchy.

This is all the more the case when one thinks that the special area of Raúl's responsibility, the defense of the state and the revolution, is the sine qua non of everything else the Revolution might stand for, since without the security that such defense efforts have given, nothing in the way of major reform could have even been attempted. And of course Fidel's passion for defense matters, the essential nature of them, his love of history and especially military history, and his own past as the military leader of the revolution in the mountains and then the comandante en jefe himself all combine to ensure that Raúl was not in any sense alone in dealing with such matters but has his brother's deep and knowledgeable interest in his area of responsibility as a given in a very day-to-day sense.

This is not to say that the two brothers were alone in this either. There is an unfortunate tendency to suggest that Fidel somehow rules alone from on high and he merely issues orders and they are carried out. This is to misunderstand the remarkable elements of the Cuban political system which, while needful of criticism on many serious matters, has as a central tenet the seeking of consensus regarding making decisions as the ideal goal across the board and does not function by any means merely on the whim of the person at the top.

In any case, we should not be surprised that until his elevation in July 2006 to the acting presidency in connection with the serious illness of Fidel, and then his formal election to the presidency in February 2008, Raúl was largely an unknown figure to the international community; this of course was less the case as regards the Cuban people and even less so as regards the security institutions of the state and especially the Fuerzas Armadas Revolucionarias. It has not been easy to do research on a man doubtless in the shadow of his immensely famous brother and who has not himself sought the limelight but rather been pleased to remain largely behind the scenes but with vital work to do. The fact that there is still no serious biography of Raúl is indicative of the difficulties in doing so. Rumor, either vitriolic diatribe or unquestioning praise, or the tendency to merely see this man as the lesser of a pair of brothers where the elder is much more important, have dominated what little work has been done on this central figure of an extraordinary if far from perfect historical experiment.

His work, as it is hoped will be shown here, he did with extraordinary impact and devotion, and he rightfully earned himself a place in the series on extraordinary reformist military figures of Latin America in the last century in which the results of the author's research were first published. It is difficult for any historian to imagine someone who has faced more difficult challenges with more success than Raúl Castro nor one who has done so under such exceptional circumstances personally, as officer, as commander, and as thinker. It is equally difficult to imagine any significant challenge to the survival of the revolutionary experiment where Raúl has not had a vital role.

This book is thus in large part the English edition of one that is part of a series on the "other" military leaders of Latin America who have not followed what most observers feel is the regional norm—that is, been commanders linked too closely, along with their institutions, to their local oligarchies, the US Embassy, and other conservative forces. Whatever their own political stances of other issues, they have been unwilling to see their armed forces trample on the popular masses or fall unquestioningly under the influence of the regional superpower and its armed forces. This series, in the words of series editor in chief Ernesto López, features several case studies of commanders and seeks to "demonstrate, in the lives of some of these leaders, in their differing objectives, methods, countries, societies and historical moments, how the military institutions lived and reacted, what were their aims, programs, methods, dreams and utopias."[1] This author will try to do this here, as well, but in this edition will add some elements not available in the Spanish edition, and will, he believes, thereby show why it is not an exaggeration to say that Raúl has truly been the architect of the Revolution's survival in the ferocious tempests it has stirred up over the last 50 years and more. If the strategist of the Revolution as a whole has unquestionably been Fidel, it will be demonstrated that *his* architect chosen to produce the strategy and armed forces to ensure that that revolution would survive was Raúl. The confidence placed in that then very young man has been clearly deserved and the Revolution, though doubtless often wounded and occasionally seemingly near death, is still very much with us. The credit for that goes in some large part to Raúl.

It is our job here to evaluate that role, not to *judge* it in moral or other terms. That the Revolution and Raúl himself have made mistakes, some of them grave, is something that both Castro brothers, and especially Fidel, have admitted on many occasions. That the understandable siege mentality of the Cuban state is unfortunate and costly in human terms, and sadly also with respect to its human rights record, is difficult to deny with any credibility at all. But this book is about Raúl as soldier of the Revolution from his early days plotting against and then opposing with arms the 1952 coup of Fulgencio Batista Zaldivar, to his training and preparation in Mexico and then his fighting under Fidel in the Sierra Maestra and, later, on his own in the northeast of Oriente province, and then his life's work as the world's longest-serving minister of defense in recent history.

While the story will often touch on the security forces more widely, this will only be done when essential to the military story itself. Here our focus will be on Raúl as soldier in the broadest sense, although it will suggest that the soldier that Raúl was has had an enormous impact on the political leader he now is. It is important to acknowledge that the threats to Cuba usually took the form of actions that were not apt to be addressed only by armed services chiefly tasked with national defense in the traditional territorial and sovereignty sense. They would rather require the development of a vast and unfortunate intelligence and security apparatus, and even a powerful and often only too ubiquitous national police force. But these other forces are not where our emphasis will lie, since in this case one is attempting to deal with the more strictly military area of Raúl's life and work. It is understood, however, that the line between military and wider security roles is often difficult to draw in any meaningful way and in Cuba and Raúl's case, more vexing than in most others one might consider.

One recognizes that this does not tell the whole story of the man as architect of the Revolution's survival, and even avoids some of the more unpleasant sides of his job as overseer of State Security services, the tasks of which were far from always savory. But space and research possibilities inside and outside Cuba limit the potential for the whole story to be told at this time and by this author. The essential elements of proving the thesis of this volume will, however, be addressed as fully as possible within the scope and space available.

A last word, then, on the subject of limitations. There is not, in the final analysis, much written on Raúl outside of either the diatribe or the excessive praise to which reference has already been made. In Cuba it is taken as a given that Raúl does not like the idea of a biography of himself, that he considers that he is merely a humble servant of the Revolution and that no such fuss is either necessary or deserved; in any case there is precious little formal information available about the man, and a proper biography, involving interviews on an extensive basis, would of course require his permission.

The job of this author has been made easier, of course, because no attempt has been made here to write a biography but rather, in the context of the series of books made reference to already, add his story to those of others such as Arbenz, Caamaño, Cárdenas, Perón, Praats, Prestes, Schneider, Seregni, and Velazco Alvarado, who have provided the basis on which one can speak of an alternate military tradition in Latin America of which that region, and its armed forces, can be justifiably proud. In the process of writing such a study, this author has counted massively on the record of his own speaking as well as his own writing and on the verbal record of hundreds of people who have spoken to him before and after he was asked to write this book.

Those who wish to write a real biography of this exceptional individual in the future, especially those who would like to use his years in the presidency as part of a full and up-to-date study of the man, will need to keep this obstacle in mind as they move forward in what is a valuable and praiseworthy objective but one with deep methodological and practical obstacles automatically associated with it.

Acknowledgments

This is not a biography of any kind, authorized or otherwise. It is a series of reflections on a person to whom I have only spoken twice, and long ago, and the story of a soldier. But the book is the result of research on and exposure to Cuba and its Revolution over more than half a century of. During those years, many people on and off the island have helped me come into a position where I could dare accept the invitation of the editor of the series on Latin American reformist senior military officers, *Otros Militares* (Other Soldiers)—in which most of the contents of this volume was first presented in Spanish—and dare to include, under my name, that of Raúl Castro. For Raúl is a serving head of state, the longest of the world's serving defense ministers in recent times, and a man widely known to Cubans and many others for his lengthy central role in the country's life. Over my time studying Cuban history, I have met literally hundreds of Cubans and others who have at least met or even known Raúl well. It is to those people, not interviewed formally but who shared their thoughts on him over the years because they knew of my interest in him as a military figure, that I owe the greatest debt of gratitude. While there is extensive (if highly dispersed) information on Raúl's military life in written form, it has been the easy informal access to the thinking of the many Cubans who have talked to me about him that has been most helpful in thinking through this subject.

On the more official side and in general on my work on Cuba, I have benefited from the assistance and good will of many persons who are working or have worked for the Cuban state, especially in the Foreign Ministry (MINREX) and the Armed Forces Ministry (MINFAR). While this has understandably been more difficult for serving regular and reserve military personnel, given the siege context in which Cuba lives, some have nonetheless had the courtesy to give me some informal thoughts, as well.

I have benefited from knowing and receiving help from many academics but beyond measure has been the friendship and support over these many years of Rafael Hernández, now editor of the prestigious journal *Temas* and one of Cuba's most important strategic thinkers. Rafael was even kind enough to look over the first draft of this book and comment on it. Another person in the same context has been Isabel Jaramillo Edwards, a tireless help for me over 15 years of work on the island's history and present. I must also mention the exceptional kindness of the late Roberto González and Francisco Pérez Guzmán, diplomat and historian respectively, who offered hospitality, deep knowledge, and friendship over several years before their untimely passings. They have been joined by many others too numerous to name, but who know who they are and, I hope, how sincere are my thanks.

In Canada, thanks go first to Dalhousie University's John Kirk, a man I view as my country's finest scholar on Cuba, and his family for their many kindnesses and for making me dare to come into the field of Cuban studies in what I hope is a serious way. Cathie Krull of Queen's University has joined their efforts in more recent years to share her insights. A list of other Canadians who know Cuba well and who helped me with my reflections would have to be headed by Juanita Montalvo of Sherritt International but would include businessmen, historians, and political scientists too numerous to name.

On the Canadian official side, I have benefited constantly from the support of the embassy in Havana and the Department of Foreign Affairs at home. My thanks go especially to Ambassadors Mark Entwhistle, Michael Small, Alex Bugailiskis, and Matthew Levin, and to the fine diplomats Paul Gibbard and Simon Cridland for all their thoughts and assistance. Defense attachés Gaëtan Tremblay, Ian Nicholls, René Gervais, the late Ross Struthers, and Laurent Caux were simply splendid backers in everything to do with this book and other research on the FAR. Marie-France Nicholls and Wanda Struthers added to this with their hospitality and charm. The mother country was also of great help in the persons of John Dew (now British ambassador to Colombia) who with his wife, Marion, took me into their residence to share thoughts. Also at the British embassy, it was a pleasure to get to know and compare notes with John Savile and Nigel Baker. Outside the official realm, I thank some of Britain's most outstanding Latin Americanists: Tony Kapcia, Jean Stubbs, Maxine Molyneux (director of the University of London's Institute for the Study of the Americas, who kindly arranged for me to spend a term there drafting this book), and Laurence Whitehead, all of whom have generously given me their ideas on this subject. In addition, I have benefited from being able to bounce thoughts off persons of the knowledge and experience including Steven Cushion, Richard Gott, Emily Morris, Paul Thompson, and Stephen Wilkinson.

They have been joined in the United States by the exceptionally generous scholars Jorge Domínguez, Richard Millett, and Frank Mora. And from elsewhere in Latin America, I would like to thank former Chilean Ambassador to Cuba Gabriel Gaspar Tapia, Raúl Benítez, Clovis Brigagão, Marcela Donadio, Rut Diamint, Juan Rial, Paz Tibuletti, and a vast range of military officers and diplomats, especially Bolivians, Ecuadoreans, Nicaraguans, and Venezuelans too extensive to name but who will know who they are.

At the Royal Military College of Canada, from which I have recently retired but where I am honored to be professor emeritus of history, I have to thank Principal Joel Sokolsky, Dean Ronald Haycock, and Professors Michael Boire, James Finan, and Brian McKercher for being not only wonderful friends but also great sounding boards for this as for so many other projects. Gord and Linda Vachon, friends to whom this book is dedicated, agreed in the case of Gord to also look over a draft of the study, and in the case of Linda, to remain patient and supportive throughout the process. To them also my gratitude for this as well as for so much else.

Chapter 1

Youth, Soldier, Officer, First Command

A Note on Youth

Raúl Castro Ruz was born on June 3, 1931, the son of Galician-born Angel Castro y Argiz and Lina Ruz González, a Cuban, and raised in relative comfort in the home of a father more than able to provide for Raúl's and his siblings' needs but whose initial connection with Cuba is rather unclear. Angel had been a soldier in the Spanish army sent to crush the rebel movement of 1895–1898 and, like many of his peers, returned to the island, following several months back in Spain, to settle there the year after the war ended. He was by all accounts proud, efficient, strong, and resourceful and soon made his way to considerable wealth and position in the region of Mayarí in Oriente province (now Holguín).

Raúl was educated at home for the first few years and then sent, as his brother Fidel had already been, to a private school in Santiago, the provincial capital. More than four years younger than Fidel, Raúl nonetheless lived alongside him for much of their childhood and watched his elder's remarkable successes, and rebelliousness, at play and at school. Smaller in stature than Fidel, Raúl did not share his brother's exceptional keenness or skill at sports but seems to have usually done tolerably well and sometimes, very well indeed, at his studies. The two brothers were close despite there being nearly five years of difference in age. Fidel repeatedly intervened with his parents through concern for his brother's well-being and the affection that has lasted a lifetime and faced uncounted tests was doubtless born in the difficult years of both their childhood.

Rather curiously for someone who was going to become the most senior soldier Cuba has ever produced, Raúl hated his period as a schoolboy in something like a military school and was expelled and sent home to an annoyed father who put him to work on his farm's accounts. He did this doubtless little knowing that this son, already clearly showing the social responsibility he was to exhibit later in life, apparently used the occasion often to foil his father's attempts to collect debts due from peasant debtors.[1] Significantly, it was not discipline that appears to have annoyed Raúl but rather the religious aspects of his studies and life at school, and what he saw as the poor quality of his instructors.

It was not long before Raúl would be in a much more real military context than a posh school with military pretensions. Active in politics from the time of his arrival for university in Havana in 1949, Raúl was as appalled as Fidel by the coup mounted by Fulgencio Batista in March 1952, which spelled the end for the corrupt *pseudo-democracy*, or what Cubans call the *pseudo-republic*, set up with US organization and bayonets over the years 1898 through1902; it was only finally formally buried with the victory of the Revolution in 1959. Raúl joined the youth wing of the communist party (Partido Socialista Popular) in that same year or early the next but at a time when Moscow was calling for gradualism and nonviolence to move Latin American states down the road to socialist opportunities.[2]

Raúl was in Europe when the movement that his brother founded— later to be styled the *26 de Julio* (July 26), at the time it was merely an armed grouping of what were largely supporters of the Ortodoxo Party—gathered steam and began to prepare for military action. He had gone there to attend a leftist youth assembly in Vienna but stayed, with financial help from his father, longer in order to spend time in other cities. No sooner did he get back, however, when, despite his party's disapproval of what it considered putschism, he joined Fidel's desperate attempt to end the tyranny of the Batista regime by sparking an insurrection through an attack on the Moncada Barracks in Santiago, Cuba's second largest military installation.

First Military Experiences

This was Raúl's first military activity. He was not in command of anything as he had gotten back from Europe so late that he was unable to be given any real training for such a role. Instead, he served as a simple soldier in a secondary attack on the military hospital, at some distance from the main barracks. He was only 22.

However, in this attack he was already showing his mettle. Not only did he by all accounts fight well and remain calm in the face of the reverses suffered by the rag-tag Fidelista force, but he also succeeded in disarming his eventual captors and escaping for a few days in an odyssey of danger before finally being recaptured and, like his brother, tried and imprisoned on the Isle of Pines (now the Isle of Youth). There, for two years, he was a crucial element in what some have considered the real beginnings of the construction of the rebel army in the training, indoctrination, and establishment of the close cadres of revolutionary fighters who were to later literally make the Revolution.

In 1955, Fidel and Raúl were amnestied but soon, under threat of assassination, fled to Mexico where they began to recruit and train the force that would return to the island in December 1956 and begin the war to end Batista's increasingly bloody dictatorship. Here Raúl again showed his skill at training and also in the implementation of a system of discipline, which, while doubtless harsh, he deemed essential if the group of armed individuals under training was to become an effective military force. It was at this time and in these circumstances that Raúl began to get something of a reputation for ruthlessness.[3] He firmly believed that without firm discipline and absolute loyalty, the movement was doomed; he therefore became a stickler for the full application of the rules, even if the results seemed unusually strict for a group of very youthful men who were not yet in any real sense soldiers.

Raúl was repeatedly given over these months responsibilities that did not seem to go well with his age. A mere 23 when he went into self-exile, he was not only frequently engaged in recruiting new elements of the group (including the later legendary Che Guevara) but also was charged with doing the reconnaissance and other key parts of the organization of the sailing of the *Granma*. This was the ill-starred small yacht that carried the 82-man expeditionary force, to Cuba's easternmost Oriente province to its disastrous landing (Che once referred to it as less a landing than a shipwreck) on December 2, 1956.

The epic story of what then happened is so extraordinary that it has become almost mythological lore in Cuba. The Batista army was alerted to the arrival of the rebels and deployed naval, air, and land assets to frustrate it. Soon after hitting the beach (it was actually a mangrove swamp two full kilometers from where Fidel intended they should land) the force was subjected to aerial attack. And on December 5, at the battle of Alegria del Pío, an army company surprised and defeated the Fidelistas and scattered them completely.

Fidel and Raúl were separated, but all knew the plan that in case of dispersal, they were to move from the lowlands south of Manzanillo to the highlands of the Sierra Maestra, Cuba's most important cordillera, and attempt to rejoin. In the attack, the rebels lost much of their equipment and most of the weapons they had worked so hard to obtain in Mexico. After 18 days of wandering, Raúl's tiny group of five found Fidel in the foothills. Fidel's first question was about how many weapons they had brought. When Raúl answered that he had five, Fidel, whose own group had two more, issued his famous excited and seemingly crazy exclamation, *"Ahora sí ganamos la guerra!"*[4]

The reunited group, still missing the bulk of its men—lost in the fighting so far—was only some 15 strong.[5] Batista had already reported the force destroyed and Fidel dead. Despite their size and quite desperate conditions, however, they soon found disenchanted peasants willing to help them on their way to the relative safety of the high Sierra Maestra. There Fidel, in classic insurgent fashion, began to train his men again and plan the small attacks that would return their confidence after the disasters so far incurred, and make them able to undertake more serious operations in the future. Raúl was in effect second-in-command at this time and was soon in his first action in La Plata, where a small military garrison was surprised and defeated by the rebels. This was followed by a series of similar small pinpricks to the Batista regime, attacks that gave the force and the young Raúl confidence, and showed their growing skill and his courage, initiative, and leadership.

From December 1956 until February 1958, Raúl's life was that of a captain in the rebel forces, moving about the cordillera trying to survive in conditions very like those experienced by previous insurgent forces of Cuba's wars for independence, and fighting when the conditions were right for it and in response to training, weapons, and morale factors of importance.[6] Fidel was very much in command, and his group was soon growing again with local farmers, long under the boot of *Batistiano* landlords, who were often willing to help and sometimes even to join the rebels. Word also spread of the seemingly miraculous survival of the landing party or at least a part of it and urban youth and farmers from other parts of the island made their way to the Sierra to join up. It was not long before more significant attacks could be launched on the army and police. And the rebel base soon boasted a small school and training center, an arms workshop and even some crops growing.

Raúl showed himself to be a good organizer, effective soldier, fine leader, and conscientious disciplinarian over this key period of the insurgency's life. He had also given special attention to the question of the *tea* or *quema de la zafra*, or setting fire to the harvest time sugarcane fields, a traditional element of revolutionary strategy going back to the wars against Spain. And it was he who on December 11, 1956, wrote to the national directorate of the movement to the effect that the application of this approach would have to be intensified, which showed that even at that stage he was involved in the political and higher strategic direction of the fighting and was not just a soldier. In addition, when a strike out of the relative safety of the Sierra and into the *llanos* (the plains to the west and north of the mountains) was required, Raúl was chosen to command it. The forces were learning about the appropriate tactics for their fight, and Raúl was becoming an experienced commander in the application of such approaches.[7]

Little wonder then that Fidel, having organized the rebels into a proper force by the late winter of 1957/8, chose Raúl to undertake what was probably the greatest single challenge the rebels then faced, other than fighting from their base in the Sierra—that of taking the uprising from the remote highlands to the lower and more populous areas of the province to the north and of founding a second front in that region. This was part of Fidel's longer-term plan, explained to Raúl in late December 1957, and would show the world that the insurrection, far from dead, was expanding and would force the army to divide its effort to dislodge it. It would follow the recent victory of Pino del Agua, which had given the rebels greater confidence and the vital captured arms that would always be their key requirement. At the same time, Juan Almeida was given the task of starting yet a third front to the west of Santiago.

Command

Both men were given the rank of *comandante*, a difficult-to-define standing roughly between captain and unit commander, like a major but eventually meaning much more, and sent on their hazardous way on March 1, 1958. Raúl's organization had received the title of *Segundo Frente Oriental* (Second Eastern Front) and Almeida's, *Tercer Frente* (Third Front), These two names would be made more personal by the addition of those of fallen heroes, in the case of Raúl's column by Frank País, the legendary martyred leader of the movement in Oriente province. This was the part of Raúl's life when he was in command of an independent fighting force, far from his brother, truly on his own in exceptionally trying conditions, organizing that force to grow and engage in serious combat against a vastly superior enemy, and making the most of his political context as well. Given the crucial importance of these months for his reputation as soldier and commander, this period will be looked at in some detail here. As we shall see, for Raúl as well as for Fidel and so many other members of the revolutionary elite, the war in Oriente molded them at least as much as their prison sentence had done their more reduced group before, and in military terms molded them even more.

Raúl was given a list of a hundred men from which he could choose his preferred 50. This is an interesting moment because later in life he was to become famous for his ability to choose the right man for the right job. A few more men were added to give him a total of 66 (only 53 had vaguely proper arms), and it was with this group, divided into four platoons, that he crossed most of an Oriente province garrisoned by several thousand troops, arriving in his assigned sector with a total of 76 men as 10 more had joined him on the march. One can imagine his feelings as he left the camp and his elder brother. He told a colleague at the time, "*Caramba, Mau, me siento como un niño que se ha desprendido del padre y ha echado a andar.*"[8] The trip was something of an epic and was the first time the rebels had used motor transport for a major part of their movements. Avoiding the enemy with skill by keeping himself well informed as to their movements and through careful planning and execution, Raúl made his way over 190 kilometers of enemy-controlled territory of which 120 were on foot.

Once in his assigned area, Raúl immediately, and with great energy, began the work of building an organization capable of survival. His first and in some ways greatest challenge proved to be not the enemy but supposedly friendly elements, independently operating *escopeteros* (light riflemen) as they were called, who in many cases were reluctant to come under Fidel's discipline, but who had been opposing the government with arms for some months. Despite the disadvantage of his highly visible youth, and without the fame of his brother, Raúl still successfully cajoled and browbeat most of them into joining the movement more formally, but some resisted all such blandishments. Independent rebel elements operating on their own could of course cause damage to the prestige of the 26 de Julio forces if their marauding had little political purpose and appeared to many to be merely another outbreak of the banditry so often present in the Cuban countryside since the mid-nineteenth century.[9] Raúl's growing strength of character and power of command showed themselves firmly here as he dealt effectively with what could have been a serious problem for Fidel's prestige and legitimacy and quite soon brought most of the rebels firmly under 26 de Julio discipline. Equally, his command became larger as groups more content with coming under his orders came in to meet him and accept their new status.

As of his first month on the ground, Raúl's front was also launching small attacks on police and army posts, as well as ones not so small, such as that on the airport of the important mining town of Moa on March 31. This was his first operation of importance where the government garrison was routed, and he then established fixed bases for future operations such as his headquarters in remote El Aguacate. He was tireless as he traveled about the sector; established linkages for logistics and recruitment; formed *Comités de Campesinos y Revolucionarios* (Revolutionary and Farmers Committees), whose job was to acquire and transport food for the rebels; structured his own command and control, intelligence, and medical services; and got to know his potential assets and challenges in this far-flung and doubtless rather lonely part of the war effort. Soon he would even be implementing a *reforma agraria* (agrarian reform) in his sector, organizing local labor, and putting into effect various revolutionary laws as well as building and operating a great many small schools and clinics.[10] Locally Raúl was becoming known as a revolutionary who got things done that were of utility to the public at large and not just to his own force. Interestingly, given his future reputation for order and good staff work he began a correspondence with higher headquarters, which meant of course his brother, which was complete and frequent, unusual characteristics for an insurgent movement in its first weeks of local deployment which would normally be characterized by sloppy military staff work.

Batista was not, however, merely waiting for the rebels to seize the initiative. It was vital to destroy this rebellion, which was increasingly attracting international attention to his corrupt and bloody regime and making essential US support for it more difficult to obtain. Taking advantage of a disastrously optimistic effort at a general strike in support of the 26 de Julio movement, one that ended in abject failure on April 9, 1958, the army launched a spring offensive the next month aimed at eliminating entirely the Fidelista threat.

At first Raúl's smaller and less important force appeared to receive little attention from the army's offensive. This was just as well as the *frente* had just been founded and early operations there, especially those in support of the general strike, had badly depleted its ammunition. It must also be said that the decision to engage the army and Guardia Rural in many places at the same time, essential if the attacks were to be of any assistance to the strike, meant that manpower in each of the chosen targets was very limited. Two of the three main attacks did not come off as planned at this time, including the one that Raúl was to lead himself. And while this was only a delay and the attacks went off successfully later on, they were too late to assist the strike. Raúl was disappointed and knew that all of this meant that the war would be much longer than optimists in the movement had thought and that therefore he would need a greater infrastructure still than the impressive but tiny one he had so far been able to put together. This was especially true in regards to weapons and ammunition. He would need a more sophisticated production capacity given the lack of weapons and munitions in general and the great difficulties of obtaining anything abroad. He soon had organized an armory, explosives factory, and a clothing and boots repair and production facility.

In any case, the delay in Batistiano attacks on the Second Front was merely a lull and only lasted for the first stages of the government offensive. Soon powerful land and air assaults were being launched against Raúl's bases in the countryside of the northeast and his troops and supporters were reeling from the blows. Aerial attacks were a particular worry as peasant morale, essential to keep his fighting force intact, fed, and supplied, was steadily worsening under their effect. This situation forced Raúl to fight in the defense of the less mobile peasantry in places and for periods not always of his choosing. Low on ammunition, with his bases under siege and major air attack, and with his peasant support base to say the least fearful, Raúl studied his options carefully and found that there were not many.[11]

Even then, however, Raúl was developing his own thinking on military matters and on his own increasingly desperate situation. As one of those taking part in the operations put it, this was now no longer traditional guerrilla war but had rather become positional warfare. And Raúl's decision was "to not yield a single inch of ground to the enemy," explaining his position thus, "The Army knows we're here, that we will defend meter by meter if he attempts to attack us, the most that can happen is that we lose the factories, but the fact is that living like nomads we won't get very far."[12]

This was exceptional fighting for a rebel force. Insurgents under this kind of pressure usually move back into more remote areas and try essentially to survive to fight on another, more propitious, day. But Raúl, in his strategy, reflected closely what was going on to the south with Fidel in that he would not move his bases, abandon his infrastructure or his peasant supporters, and in this went even further than Fidel was doing in the Sierra.

Then Raúl, on June 22, made the decision that was to launch his name onto the international stage as never before. In order to stop the air attacks on his troops and the peasant population he staged *Operación Anti-Aérea* (Operation Anti-Air), the kidnapping four days later of a group of 24 US Marine Corps personnel and of 25 US managers and employees of US-owned businesses, and followed this with a warning that further air attacks would place in danger the lives of the kidnapped.[13] This garnered US attention as nothing in the war had done so far, and pressure on Batista from Washington was fierce. Havana promptly ceased the aerial bombardments in the zone and gave Raúl breathing space to reorganize and revitalize his command as well as regain peasant confidence in his survivability and chances of eventual victory. The stroke, however, had not been authorized by Fidel and led to some harsh words from higher headquarters. Whether under the conditions of the time Raúl could have consulted Fidel on his decision is a matter of debate to this day. But what is not debated is the courage and audacity of the actions taken by a local commander, who had just celebrated his twenty-seventh birthday a few days before, and the general success of the strategy of positional warfare adopted.

Raúl's reputation within the rebel movement soared with the success of Operación Anti-Aérea. And when Fidel's main force drove back the main offensive against him in the Sierra Maestra, the pressure eased on Raúl's Second Front as well, and the stage was set for a new phase of the war. Fidel ordered the preparation of his own invasion of the west of the island, following on the traditions of the historic invasion of 1895 that eventually resulted in independence. This would be conducted by two more comandantes, Che Guevara and Camilo Cienfuegos, and would start off toward the west in short order once the government offensive was driven back. Fidel would meanwhile launch the eastern end of that offensive with his own forces and those of his other columns.

For Raúl the orders were to increase offensive operations with a view to the total defeat of government forces in the northeast of Oriente and eventually the surrounding of Santiago. In order to do this, he built up the hitting power of his forces by widespread recruitment, setting up an even larger training and education centre for the Second Front; schools; more small factories for things needed for operations including very light weapons, uniforms, explosives, and ammunition; a more formal Intelligence Officers Corps specializing in interrogating prisoners of war; a further intelligence service to include early warning about enemy aircraft raids that was based on peasant supporters; an inspectorate; a personnel department; a radio and propaganda section; police; and the lightest of air forces.

This last idea, surely one of his most original, led to the formation of the *Fuerza Aérea Rebelde* (Rebel Air Force), a group of light aircraft eventually reaching seven in total, which were bought or commandeered from a variety of sources or actually captured from Batista's own forces and which operated in essentially logistics support roles for Raúl. Moreover, by late in 1958 he was in a position to use his two very light combat aircraft to assist in the capture of an enemy garrison through bombing it from above.[14] Raúl's growing reputation for thinking in an innovative fashion was enhanced even more.

If this was true of the military side of the picture, it was equally so of the political. In his part of *Cuba Libre*, (the name given to areas liberated from Batista as it had been given by the insurgents to their freed areas in the war for independence), Raúl had by late 1958 functioning elements of government not only for his troops but for the public in his zone, including departments of war, justice, propaganda, health, finance, public works and communications, and education, as well as agrarian and labor bureaus. There was not only a radio set up by the front but also a small newspaper, *Segundo Frente*, and the agrarian and labor bureaus served as liaisons between military command and related sectors in liberated areas. And lest these efforts be considered more propagandistic than real, it should be noted that there were some 400 teachers and 160 total medical workers and support staff operating in the Second Front's version of Cuba Libre.

This allowed Raúl to host in September 1958 a *Congreso Campesino en Armas* (Congress of Farmers in Arms) where farmers expressed both their frustrations with the conditions under which they lived and worked and their hopes for agrarian reform extended from their region to the nation as a whole once the war was won. And, although there were similar initiatives and departments in other parts of the liberated zones, all authors agree that in Raúl's sector the organizations were more solid and developed than anywhere else. In December, he was also able to host a *Congreso Obrero en Armas* (Congress of Workers in Arms) that served similar roles to that of the agricultural workers earlier on.

It is also of interest to mention that Raúl himself served as a teacher at the *Escuela para Maestros de las Tropas José Martí* (José Martí School for Teachers of Troops), a school he set up personally with a distinct political purpose. He himself found time to teach a course in ethics of the combatant and also oversaw the other subjects including history, geography, civics, and objectives and problems of the Cuban Revolution. His troops came from a wide variety of backgrounds and while almost all were of humble origin; among them were a few professionals and students, some small and even medium bourgeois, housewives, the unemployed, farmers and agricultural laborers, and many others. Most came from the surrounding countryside and local cities such as Santiago and Guantánamo. Many were illiterate, so the work to be done by the teachers was taxing indeed.[15] News of what was going on inside Cuba Libre reached out widely and had great political impact in a nation such as Cuba and especially a region such as Oriente.

Raúl is widely reported to have appeared to be everywhere at the same time, coordinating his various columns, taking command in individual actions especially when his steadying hand was needed, and keeping going an active headquarters and local political and administrative system, while working particularly hard to bring in essential and difficult-to-obtain arms from abroad.[16] The steady and impressive growth of his force eventually allowed Raúl to break it up into a series of six separate columns that spread out over his zone of action. The fighting in the sector became very widespread in the last two months of 1958, and he coordinated the attacks on garrisons, small towns, villages, police stations, and even navy shipping. He had not given ground, even under the heaviest army pressure in the summer, since he felt that his infrastructure was the key to his success and essential to maintaining an effective presence in the area as well as pressure on the enemy, and he was not going to do so now. He had seized the initiative in his area entirely by the last weeks of the war.

As early as the second week of November, his successes were so troubling to the army in his zone that a report from the commander of the Seventh Military District to the director of operations of the general staff of the army, under the title *Informe sobre Guerrilleros de Raúl Castro Ruz* (Report on the Guerrillas of Raúl Castro Ruz), stated that he "has a force of not fewer than three thousand men, well armed, with abundant ammunition and food."[17] This was at a time when the whole of the rebel army, on all its fronts, could not possibly have been very close to this figure, and when Raúl still faced vast problems of weapons and ammunition acquisition. The Second Front had become a threat to Batista's control of Oriente, almost as serious as Fidel's own in the south.

When Batista fled Havana on the night of December 31, 1958, Raúl's forces were already assisting Fidel in placing the ring around Santiago that was to lead to its fall—the capital was taken over the next two days. He was then given the key job of effecting the surrender of the Moncada Barracks, which could have been crucial to efforts by the army and US embassy to abort the victory at this vital juncture.

When Fidel left Santiago for his Caravan of Liberty, the famous victory drive across almost the whole of Cuba to Havana, which culminated in his reaching the newly liberated city on January 8, it was Raúl who was left in charge of Santiago and Oriente province as his elder brother took on the vastly difficult job of bringing order to the capital's many rebel elements, and putting an end to army plotting with the US embassy to stop his triumph. Raúl's central importance could hardly have been clearer because at this crucial juncture in the Revolution it could still only be said that Oriente had actually been won militarily and was safe for the rebels. Everything else was still in the air. Raúl's role in clearing that air was to be even more impressive than the one he had played so far. And at only 27 he was already a successful commander in his own right as well as one of the most respected leaders in the victorious 26 de Julio movement.

To recap what had been happening, this extraordinarily young and relatively inexperienced commander had taken a small group of rebel troops, themselves having little experience and poorly armed, to another part of the country and against all odds had established a headquarters and fighting columns to make war on an enemy vastly more powerful; had calmed and brought under discipline bandit elements in his sector; had made fast a network of connections with the peasantry and workers in the area in which his forces operated; had established a number of factories, schools, and clinics that made his area of the country a haven and beacon for others; and had produced a functioning command in the midst of the ferocious attack of government forces. He had shown even further courage under fire, the first requirement for having the respect of other military personnel, and the ability to make decisions not only under such circumstances but also in the difficult day-to-day context of command, and had forged his own Cuba Libre in northeastern Cuba. He had taken one difficult and risky tactical and even strategic decision after another in this campaign and had clearly if not on every occasion rewarded Fidel's confidence in him.

This was no minor leader or someone merely chosen for command responsibility because he was the brother of the most senior commander. This was a proven commodity, a commander of valor, skill and value recognized even by the rank and file of the rebel army who sought to find ways to serve under him.[18] He was given a terribly difficult job and did it well. The enemy was numerous and well-armed, the local forces were ill-disciplined and lacking in cohesion, the terrain challenging and treacherous, the enemy's friends all around and powerful, and the peasantry on whom one had to depend uncertain and especially at first, often skeptical as to the chances of a rebel victory. Careful planning, courageous and correct decision-making, organization, bravery, and intelligence transformed this negative tactical and strategic context into one of victory. He had also founded a leadership cadre locally, which in many senses was already showing signs of becoming a real officer corps, capable of winning battles and conducting operations with not only military skill but also political acumen.

Some twelve thousand square kilometers of territory had been freed by the Segundo Frente, and Raúl had been in overall or direct command of 248 operations, big and small. Three air raids and a great many supply missions had been undertaken by his air force that had been at first considered by most as rather a mad idea. His troops had shot down three enemy aircraft and had cost Batista's forces nearly two thousand casualties—killed, wounded, and prisoners—taken 25 garrisons or headquarters, captured 6 aircraft, taken over 16 trains, and obtained around 1,000 weapons.[19] Only one man can claim overall this success although obviously his soldiers, subordinate commanders, and elder brother's mantle made it possible.

Chapter 2

Minister but Still a Soldier

The situation in early January 1959 requires some description at this stage. The Batista army, *Guardia Rural*, police and security services were still formally in existence although essentially broken as fighting forces. The US embassy in Havana was still divided as to how best to handle the arrival of Fidel and his *barbudos* in the capital although Washington was moving towards physical elimination of the problem as the best solution.[1] The oligarchy was troubled but largely passive, hoping doubtless to control any potential reform excesses the still largely unknown Fidel might be planning—although this was already starting to look difficult with Fidel's repeated calls for vast and sweeping change in Cuba as he spoke at various mass meetings on his way to Havana. The bulk of the middle class appears to have been of guarded support for someone they tended to see as radical but not a major threat to those economically below the traditional ruling elite. And the peasantry and the working classes, to the extent they had a voice, were little less than ecstatic about the reformers getting to power.

At the same time, major elements of the opposition to Batista still remained in an uncertain connection with the 26 de Julio movement with some university groups, and the impressive *Directorio Revolucionario*, not necessarily entirely won over. Fidel had to address all manner of threats to his victory then as army plotters, recalcitrant opposition elements, US diplomats and military mission officers, former politicians of the corrupt pseudo-republic days, and others sought to influence or indeed frustrate the wider reform ideas of the rebel movement.

While dealing with all this, Raúl became both a member of the "shadow government" (a civilian formal government had taken over officially but real power seemed squarely in the hands of the *Ejército Rebelde* and its comandantes) and responsible for reorganizing that force while holding on to yet another job in maintaining the links with Oriente. He was at this stage the most frequently traveling member of a very mobile government dashing back to the east whenever needed there.

If ever the "otherness" of this officer or his armed forces were to be obvious it was at this time, although as will be seen this state of affairs was to become a constant with him and his forces over several decades. With the flight in the weeks after early January not only of the dictator himself, but also of the senior members of his bureaucracy and officer corps, and many other administrators at various levels, Cuba and its new government were left with a desperate lack of qualified personnel just at a time when they hoped to implement the major reforms that were promised since the time of Fidel's famous 1953 "History Will Absolve Me" speech during his trial for leading the Moncada attack of that July. Fidel intended to virtually immediately put into practice many of those ideas, as he had recently promised on the march to Havana. In particular he wished to give relief to the citizenry in the areas of rent controls and electricity prices, and of course he was keen to get on with the Latin American dream of effective agrarian reform.

In order to implement such a program, however, he needed trusted cadres of people who could manage large schemes. And this was not available in any sector of the Cuban population of the time given the flight of so much of the managing class. Thus, Fidel turned to the armed forces to give him the loyal if not particularly trained personnel to carry out the reform package. What its officers, NCOs and even soldiers lacked in administrative skills they more than made up for, in the eyes of Fidel, with their loyalty to him personally and their devotion to the cause of deep reform of the Cuban polity.[2]

While a defense minister, Dr Augusto Martínez Sánchez, had been named as part of the liberal cabinet put into place in January, Fidel remained as commander-in-chief of the Ejército Rebelde, and Raúl, as second-in-command, was steadily given more direct control of the day-to-day operations of that force. At the same time, the purge of the armed forces of the dictatorship began with Fidel and Raúl retaining only those elements with unquestionably popular credentials and no taint of having been involved in war crimes such as torture and the summary execution of combatants or aerial bombardment of civilian populations—so much a part of the Batista regime and its way of maintaining control of the public and making war.

The idea of a civilian government made up of dignitaries from the old Cuba was not well seen by Raúl, a view he expressed even before it was named or the war was won. When chosen, it was made up of some individuals he distrusted, who soon proved unwilling to put into place the radical reforms Fidel had in mind. As the only real power behind the new government, Fidel took over the prime ministry (with Raúl now as commander of the Ejército Rebelde) in February.[3] Changes were now pushed in earnest across the board, with the rebel army given key roles in almost all of them, especially nationalization of the dictator's properties (and those of his closest colleagues), telephone and rent reform, the making public of beach access, agrarian reform, the Ministry of Agriculture, fisheries, airlines, and a host of other fields of government.

Raúl now came into his own as a military leader of not only the whole defense establishment of his country but also of that organization at a time when it was being asked to take on numerous roles that were not considered normal or traditional in Latin American, or indeed most other, armed forces. It became clear in the first few months of the revolutionary government that this was not going to be a typical Latin American revolution, where nothing really changed except the names of those in charge. Rather it was aimed at being a revolutionary transformation of society across the board, and thus the man who was given the task of defending it from its growing and increasingly ferocious opponents was not, could not be, a Latin American military officer of the classic type. Raúl was now to show that not only in the field but also now in government he was indeed a different type of Latin American military man. He was to be shown to be the willing leader of the armed forces of a revolutionary state, armed forces with roles of a revolutionary kind when compared with the Latin American norm, and armed forces devoted to the revolutionary project of which Fidel was leader and inspiration. It was in this very special context that Raúl was to become *the* chief military architect of the system of protection of that project and for much of its implementation, as well.

So How Different Was He?

This is perhaps a good moment to look back and ask in what senses Raúl was different from previous Cuban senior officers and especially from the commanders of Cuba's military as they had evolved from colonial times to the present. As we have just seen, Raúl Castro could fulfill the revolutionary responsibilities given to him by the *comandante en jefe* because he was of course in no sense a "normal" Latin American military officer. It is clear that in his fighting in the guerrilla war as a rebel commander he used highly unorthodox methods to win. But in this and his new roles, how did he differ from what one had come to expect in Cuba and in the region?

The colonial experience of Cuba had been truly exceptional. This was the only part of the vast Spanish imperial domains that was never to have a civilian governor even in peacetime. The nature of the island's role in the imperial system did not allow for such a luxury. For it was Havana's magnificent port that had given Cuba its development and special place in the empire as well as its name of *clave de un imperio* (key to an empire). It was in the harbor there, protected from hurricanes as few others by its long narrow entrance way, its surrounding hills, and its great size—and from external attack by these same features and by easily commanding fortresses and castles still to be seen today—that the vital treasure fleets of Spain's American empire assembled.[4] To Havana came ships from Peru, Mexico, and Cartagena de Indias on the northern tip of South America, which then waited in the harbor for the arrival of the fleet of naval ships that would convoy them, hopefully safely, to Spain in the face of pirates, corsairs, and occasional regular naval attack from the empire's numerous and envious enemies.

That Havana sat astride the finest and most rapid winds and currents that could speed those ships eastward to Spain merely ensured that no other port in the Americas was as essential to the mother country as it. It was no surprise that the city was soon large and prosperous, and fortified and garrisoned like no other in the Americas.[5]

Garrisoned as it was, however, by regular imperial troops, it still fell to determined British assault in 1762; this shattering event for imperial morale led to a complete rethinking of colonial military administration in its aftermath. Cuba became the test case for a series of measures, forced on Madrid by the changing strategic context dominated by absolute British naval mastery, aimed at making the colonies take on the bulk of the responsibility for colonial defense. In part this was a result of the fine showing given by Cuban militiamen in the failed but spirited guerrilla defense of Havana during the British siege.[6] The tradition of guerrilla war is in this sense born as of this time and is only reawakened in Cuban military history in the independence wars against Spain and later in the revolutionary war waged by Fidel Castro.

The *criollo* (native) officer corps of these colonial forces was, however, typical of the Spanish empire at the time; conservative, aristocratic, unprofessional, and from the dominant classes of their society. The later experience of the Ten Year's War (1868–1878) and the War of Independence (1895–1898) meant that a vast number of Cubans served with one side or the other in the fighting, and thousands of officers over that time got exposure to combat. Despite this, it was only when the United States intervened in the latter war that victory was quickly achieved, and that victory was far from complete for Cubans who had fought for the goal of independence and found themselves well short of that objective. Four years of US occupation ensued and during this crucial period the US organized a Rural Guard with some attributes of an army but with the essential role of keeping order in the countryside, thus protecting growing and massive US investments on the island, encouraged and given special advantages during the occupation, and ensuring Cuba remained under US domination even after any future military withdrawal.[7]

This Rural Guard remained until 1959 in one form or another but a regular army had been set up in 1909, expanded in both world wars especially the second, and soon became a key arbiter, as in so much of Latin America, of the country's political life. Politicians maneuvered for military support as essential for survival in power, with the inevitable results on the potential professionalization of the institution that one had been led to expect in most of the region. US domination of the forces remained total and was reinforced by successive military interventions and occupations, the strategic importance of the island in the Second World War leading to very close cooperation in that conflict, the Mutual Assistance Pact signed with Washington as a result of the Korean War of 1950 through1953, the basing arrangements the United States enjoyed in the country as a pre-condition of granting independence in 1902/3, and the long series of US military missions (army, navy, and air force) of size and influence sent to the island over those decades. This connection was extended even further during the *batistiato* even though at its end, there was a partial US arms embargo in place which showed that even so close a connection had limits.[8]

The officer corps was not untypical of Central American and Caribbean armed forces either, although in many respects it was rather different from some South American armies. Officers were highly conscious of their political power, and considered themselves the embodiment of what was best in the nation, feeling that their institution was the key to nation-building and nationalism. They tended to have an exaggerated sense of patriotism, at least in their public pronouncements, while in reality they were overwhelmingly tied to the US armed forces. Distant from the oligarchy in social origins and education but tied to them by mutual interest and a desire to survive and prosper; the Cuban officer corps was thus almost automatically bloated, spoiled by its political partners, sought after by all, and self-perpetuating.

Cuban senior officers had of course begun their careers in the traditional officer cadet schools known throughout the region and had therein been the objects of real attempts to inculcate higher values of self-sacrifice, austerity, and the simple life. They tended to be from families that were military by tradition and divided themselves into *camarillas* (small interconnected clannish groupings) of like-minded and mutually reinforcing groups of officers connected through any number of ways to the oligarchy. Their rise to high military positions, and their social advancement, was during the period before the Batista seizure of power in March 1952—and closely linked to the periodic coups that rocked the Republic over the first half of the nineteenth century. The nature of the Batista regime was rather different from that which had come before.

Batista had been something of the strongman of Cuba, although in different ways over these years of change, since his meteoric rise from stenographer sergeant to commander-in-chief in large part as a result of his role in the 1930s revolutionary overthrow of the Machado dictatorship and its sequels. Retiring from effective power to Florida from 1944 to 1948, he then returned in order to set up his own political party and prepare to run for president in the next elections. As it became ever more certain that there was no way in which such a result could come his way, he engineered with officers loyal to him the coup of 1952 which again vaulted him into power and with him those officers who had backed him in the undertaking.

A large number of the senior officers had come from the junior ranks during the troubled 1930s and were not from the traditional families that had tended to provide most of the officer corps up to that time. Most officers were from the prosperous west of Cuba and almost all were white in a country where a huge percentage of the population was *mulato* or black; there was not a single officer who was black. All were married to women of similar social origins, most had criminal records—although often for minor misdemeanors— most had taken at least one military course in the United States, and all were formally Roman Catholic.

That, however, was where their homogeneity ended. For the nature of the convulsions of the 1930s meant that their rise to senior rank was only as a result of their support for Batista during those years and afterward. This became even more the case with the almost incredibly rapid rise in rank of those willing to support the dictator in the later coup. Few officers *de academia* (that is, graduates of the military college) survived these changes, and the senior ranks after 1952 were dominated by those who exhibited only *el afán de lucro y violencia.*[9]

It would be hard to imagine anyone less at home in the environment of these senior officers than Raúl. While many of them in some way came from the lower middle class and the ranks of the NCOs of the 1930s, they were as a group ignorant, vulgar, steeped in institutional and personal violence, self-satisfied politically and as individuals, and generally without values or positive goals related to their profession of arms or even the nation. They in essence were not military men at all.[10] Raúl in contrast may not have been a traditional Latin American military man, but he was a proven military man and leader of his own making and his own mind.

It must have been satisfying if challenging for Raúl to undertake the purging of essentially all of these commanders of the regular army and see his own tried and true Ejército Rebelde replace that corrupt and inefficient institution. For with very few exceptions indeed, these senior officers were sacked, and most soon chose self-exile. On the other hand, many had been involved in torture and significant repression, including aerial bombardment of civilian populations. For them the firing squad or very lengthy sentences in prison waited. Raúl and other officers of the Ejército Rebelde had among their other responsibilities the organization and implementation of these sentences, and it must be said that over time some of the trials had a "kangaroo" element to them. A number of police and army officers were humiliated and browbeaten during some of the trials bringing what were probably the earliest international complaints about the Revolution. And while some of those complaints were doubtless self-serving and cynical, it was difficult to deny that the conduct of the trials was on occasion, to say the least, unfortunate.

Few doubted the guilt of the convicted, but more than a few complained about the indignity of some of the proceedings. Fidel was able to call on moderate and prestigious judges for most of the trials, but suggestions by him that revolutionary justice was not about legal precepts but rather morality offended many who otherwise supported not only the Revolution but also the need for swift and exemplary justice being meted out to criminal elements of the former regime. The United States found its first real whip with which to beat Castro on the human rights front. It would not be the last.

Raúl's prestige in particular, as head of the armed forces and as often appearing to be especially intransigent about the trials, suffered. But it must be remembered to what degree the commanders of the Ejército Rebelde had themselves suffered losing so many of their friends to enemy torture and brutality over such a long time, going back to the hours immediately after the 1953 Moncada attack when so many of the prisoners were killed after surrender and usually after frightful torture. It is also the case that throughout the war in the mountains rebel prisoners virtually never survived capture by government forces. Even so some 550 former army, Guardia Rural, *Policía Nacional*, and secret police personnel were executed over these early years, a high figure even by most Latin American revolutionary standards.[11]

Raúl's background, as we have seen, could hardly have been more different from this pre-Castro Cuban military norm. Coming from a reasonably well-to-do if farming family in the east, attending good private schools, but soon and often rebelling against authority, Raúl had little military background in his environment. His love for organization and order, discipline and structures came rather from the clear need he saw for such things if victory was to be achieved in the long struggle against Batista and then in the fight for the survival of the revolutionary experiment that continues today. As of early 1959, the romantic insurgent struggle was over and the perhaps more difficult one of organizing the defense of the Revolution against its massive and myriad enemies began.

It would be wrong to leave this discussion of otherness without mentioning that the nature of the Ejército Rebelde and of Raúl himself deserves some attention in this context. Raúl was not just a rebel officer of a rebel army. He was Raúl Castro, a specific rebel officer and from a very specific rebel army.

Fidel had after the Moncada events understood better than ever that the Batista dictatorship could only be overthrown by a proper armed force able to conduct operations of a truly military kind. While he was certainly overly optimistic about the likelihood of the landing of December 1956 sparking a widespread, even national, insurgency, he did know very well that without an insurgency Batista would simply not fall.[12] Everything we see of his conduct of the planning and organization in prison, even more the training in Mexico, and finally the handling of training and offensive and defensive operations in the Sierra Maestra, places the emphasis on the proper discipline, structures, hierarchy, training, and conduct expected of a real army.

The Ejército Rebelde was certainly not a regular army, but it was not a hodgepodge either. Rather it was disciplined, organized, hierarchical, trained, and handled as a proper army. Fidel was a stickler for discipline as hundreds of personal accounts show, and Raúl was at least as much so. The reporting system Raúl had in place in the north of Oriente is much more similar to that of a regular army than to that in many such formal military organizations. It is not too much to say that in many senses the Ejército Rebelde had rather more of the intangible but important things that go into making up an army than did the national armed forces loyal to Batista. And Fidel and Raúl must be given the credit for this, although more so the overall commander Fidel, anchored as he was in years of close study and love of military history.[13]

Likewise Raúl may have been a *revolutionary* officer and soldier, but he was unquestionably an officer and soldier. He expected to obey and be obeyed. He did not ask others to take risks he was not willing to take himself. He was stern but listened to others when a commander is expected to listen to those under him. He was personally disciplined and expected the same from his troops. He was also loyal not only up the chain of command to his commander but also down that chain to his subordinates. If compared with his regular counterparts, one could easily come to the conclusion that he was much more of an officer, in the full and positive sense of the word, than most of them.

Named Minister and "Promoted"

By the end of the summer of 1959, the need to defend the revolutionary experiment was obvious to all in the new government. While Fidel had at first planned on maintaining a much smaller military establishment than Batista's, perhaps only some sixteen thousand personnel, by September US opposition to his regime had solidified and was beginning to take subversive and military directions. At the same time the reforma agraria, presented in the spring of that year, had caused a massive reaction on the part of the land-owning classes who feared for their lands and power. This was complicated by the enormous role that US citizens had in agricultural land ownership on the island, the inheritance of the repeated military occupations the republic had known since 1898. The honeymoon had well and truly come to an end with armed opposition groups forming in several parts of the country, self-exile undertaken by tens of thousands from the oligarchy and upper middle classes (and increasing every week), and a government sliding steadily to the left. In August, a Czech commercial mission visited Havana as part of a discreet attempt to reduce the negative effects of the deteriorating relationship with the United States, Cuba's largest commercial partner by far, by establishing economic links with the Soviet bloc; at the same time Che Guevara visited communist Yugoslavia. US military missions were at first ignored by the new government, then reduced in size; all formal military connection was of course severed in January 1961 when Washington broke diplomatic relations.

In September of 1959, Raúl dispatched the first military mission to visit both the Soviet Union and China which, it must be said, received scant attention from either country's armed forces—though the latter did include an interview with Mao Tse-tung. And at home the links between the 26 de Julio and the Partido Socialista Popular were becoming more formal and stronger.[14] Little wonder that tongues were wagging in Washington about dangerous trends on the island, calls for unseating the revolution were increasing, and planning to effect such a goal was begun in earnest. Under these circumstances, a small armed force for the defense of the revolutionary project was no longer a logical option, and Cuba began serious planning to defend island and regime.

Tasked with undertaking the organization of this new defense structure was Raúl, now 28, named the next month the minister of the Revolutionary Armed Forces, as the new post was to be termed, and later given the heretofore unknown title of *general de ejército* (general of the army). His initial activity was exceptional. He sent a military equipment and armaments purchasing mission to Europe that very month, and his other planned reforms were drastic indeed. The ministry of defense as well as the army, navy, and air force of the Republic were all disbanded by Laws 599 and 600 the next month. The new *Ministerio de las Fuerzas Armadas Revolucionarias* (Ministry of the Revolutionary Armed Forces or MINFAR) was established with the *Fuerza Aérea Rebelde* and *Marina de Guerra Rebelde* joining the Ejército Rebelde with legal status. The same law reorganized the police, with the old Policía Nacional being replaced by the *Policía Nacional Revolucionaria* (National Revolutionary Police or PNR). Other security forces would be organized in the next years to handle counter-revolutionary subversion, defend the leadership from assassination attempts, and fight terrorism and all would respond through a chain of command that passed through Raúl as minister of the Fuerzas Armadas Revolucionarias.

Raúl was not at all pleased to find himself as a minister after being in military command of the armed forces since February, when his brother became prime minister. He feared that his job would become a bureaucratic one. But there is no sign that this happened. In a first public statement as minister, Raúl made clear an approach to defense which has not wavered in a half-century and which showed he was far from becoming a boring bureaucrat: "We will never be satisfied until through our organization and always counting on the unsubstitutable collaboration of the people of Cuba, our country is in conditions to make itself respected militarily by the small and the strong."[15]

But the job to be done was huge. What was to be done with the thousands of personnel of Batista's armed forces? How was one to manage the incorporation into the FAR of the personnel who had done such a good job fighting the tyranny in the Directorio Revolucionario? What kind of armed forces could be built up in a small and poor country—poorer than ever with the flight of the dictator with such a significant part of the national treasury—when the country to be deterred from attack and subversion was the greatest power in the history of the world and sitting a mere 150 kilometers from the island? Where could arms be obtained for such deterrence in a world terrified by a US negative reaction to the selling of such weapons to an ostracized Cuba? How could one find the officers for such a large force and provide that force with an adequate body of senior NCOs when the FAR was at the same moment being asked to produce personnel for the running of so much of the national economy and administration?[16]

This list of challenges would have daunted anyone, but Raúl went about calmly addressing them, to the extent he could, one by one. Raúl's nomination, however, brought about an even more immediate crisis since elements of the Ejército Rebelde were already worried about what they saw as the drift to communism by the new regime; the naming of Raúl, one of the few more or less open communists in the new government, sparked a showdown with personnel headed by comandante Hubert Matos Benítez, the commanding officer of the armed forces in the central province of Camaguey. These men presented their resignations separately but at the same time in an act of insubordination that Raúl could not accept as anything but a show of force and an attempt to moderate the Revolution from inside its most important institution, the one expected to be the most disciplined. He had to act and act quickly, which he did.

Raúl dispatched the already legendary comandante Camilo Cienfuegos to relieve Matos of his command. And Fidel called on loyalist units of the police and army to stand ready to defend the Revolution if the units under Matos's command attempted a political move. In the midst of it all, a dissident air force officer flew his plane from Florida to drop anti-Fidel leaflets over the capital. Fidel then felt that he had to go to Camaguey himself to put an end to an event that still sparks emotion in Cuba and about which we are unlikely ever to know the complete truth. What was clear, however, is that this was as close a call as the Revolution was ever to have from inside the ranks of its own armed forces and it was perhaps not surprising that the much criticized Revolutionary Tribunals were brought back on a more permanent basis at this time.[17]

Raúl's nomination as minister of the armed forces remained, and Che Guevara, one of the few other known communists in the movement, was quickly named president of the National Bank. The regime needed the communists to help run programs that could not be managed by neophytes or just the hard-pressed armed forces. And as we have seen the drift to the left, even on the international level, was well on its way. It is the view of this author, in this extremely politicized debate, that it is probable that this was neither Fidel's intention earlier on nor the necessarily inevitable direction he would have taken at this time. But visceral US opposition to his reforms, and its combination with strident upper-class rejection of them, was too powerful and dangerous a union for him to remain without allies other than just the armed forces and a diffuse peasantry and working class. The USSR internationally and the PSP at home would have to be sought as important sources of help in the challenges to come.

A First Popular Militia

It does not come as a surprise to think that under these circumstances Fidel and Raúl should be thinking of expanding the armed forces. As mentioned, the problem was how to do so without the unthinkably high costs of a larger regular force, in terms of both the personnel and financial resources of the nation. The threat from the United States was clear to all, as was that of the domestic rightist reaction, and there was enormous popular interest in defending the Revolution. This was particularly clear in the peasant reaction to the Agrarian Reform but was also so among the members of the growing women's movement.[18] A popular militia seemed the only way forward in answering the challenges of revolutionary defense, and Raúl was given the job of founding such an institution in the midst of such busy times along lines often suggested by Fidel.

Thus were born the *Milicias Nacionales Revolucionarias* (National Revolutionary Militias or MNR) although it should be said that in the usual way of those extraordinary days, this was less structured and thought out than one might think many years later. As early as August 1959, a small squad of 12 pro-revolutionary peasants, calling themselves *Los Malagones* (Malagon's boys), was given the job of finding and eliminating a small band of counterrevolutionaries who had risen in arms in a remote area of the westernmost province of Pinar del Rio under the command of an ex-Batista army corporal. In a few days, the business was over with such éclat that Fidel, upon hearing the news, exclaimed, "*Ahora sí habrá milicias en Cuba*" (Now there really will be militias in Cuba).[19]

It should first be made clear to what extent the building of this force was in and of itself a revolutionary step for Fidel to take and for Raúl to try to follow up.[20] Even the idea of popular militias in Latin America had not had a happy history as witnessed by events in Guatemala and Bolivia earlier in the decade and in Haiti and Mexico earlier in their independent histories, as well as was to be seen later on in Chile and Nicaragua in the 1970s. The powerful armies of Latin American countries have rarely wished to share the position of unique legitimate source of the use of force with anyone else and least of all with half-trained and often, to them, politically dubious militias.

This was, however, far from the case in Cuba. The Ejército Rebelde was in no way a traditional Latin American force jealous of its position and privileges. Instead it was the armed element of a revolutionary project under the leadership of a proven military commander and charismatic figure, Fidel Castro. Few in an army of ex-jungle warriors and ex-urban fighters were likely to complain about getting help from other members of the very society and social classes from which they had so recently come. And while Raúl's early order as minister that the army's troops cut off their beards and adopt normal military haircuts did make the army look more professional, most rebel officers had been expecting to go back to civilian life immediately after victory. Only Fidel's often very personal appeal that they stay in the ranks to defend the Revolution against its enemies and organize and implement its reforms kept many of them from leaving the forces altogether.[21]

The excellent analyst and philosopher María del Pilar Díaz Castañón refers to the foundation of the militia in the autumn of 1959 as "*la obra más típica de la joven revolución*" (the most typical oeuvre of the young revolution), doubtless meaning by that its representation of popular generosity, the new work ethic of self-abnegation and service to society, and the need to do worthwhile things (such as being a part-time soldier) that would have been simply unthinkable before 1959 in Cuba.[22] Equally unthinkable, women were to form a major part of the organization and, in keeping with their role in the Sierra, were to train to fight and not just to be nurses, administrators, typists, and the like.[23] Raúl was indeed, under Fidel's inspiration and close supervision, creating something very much other than Latin American norms.

The issue soon became, now that one was going to have a mass force which must not cost very much, how to arm it. And once again, US unwillingness to sell Fidel any weapons or equipment was coupled with active diplomacy to ensure that no US ally did so either. Despite some weapons obtained from Belgium (FN 7.62 rifles arrived in some numbers in October 1959 but mostly under a contract signed with the Batista government) and one or two non-NATO sources, in general this first US "embargo" of Cuba, that on weaponry, worked very well.[24] This meant, of course, that given the perception of both internal and external threat, Cuba would have to look elsewhere than to the United States and Western Europe. And with time it did.

Cuba thus sought its first purchases of weapons from the Eastern bloc, especially from Czechoslovakia. Havana was interested in anti-tank weapons, light infantry arms, mortars, antiair systems, and other weapons that would be needed to repel an invasion by both sea and air. Moscow of course had such systems as did its allies but moved in a measured fashion and quite carefully in fulfilling Cuba's requests in the light of potential negative US reactions and growing distrust of where Fidel was taking Cuba at this time. [25]

Leaving ideas of a small army behind, Fidel and Raúl moved to establish a militia that would reportedly reach nearly two hundred thousand in strength and a regular army of just under twenty-five thousand. These figures should be taken with some reserve because some of the bandying about of such numbers was doubtless related to the idea of deterring the United States from attack while trying to overawe upper-class resistance to the Revolution. But certainly a major force was being set up to complement the regulars themselves who were probably not purged as fiercely as they might have been as a result of the need for a reasonable number of them to stay on with the new and much larger national armed forces.

The basic lines of the strategy of national defense, and of deterrence, that would last to this day can already be seen in these changes. Here is its first manifestation. It had proven impossible to effect major reforms without stimulating the hostility of the United States and that rejection was increasingly taking strident form. And the drift into the Soviet orbit, itself occasioned in large part by that US hostility, acted in a vicious circle to provide even more hostility on the part of Washington to virtually anything the revolutionary government proposed. The bilateral relationship spiraled downwards.

For Raúl, however, the key was that recruits were flocking to the Colors and were, in their tens of thousands, only too willing to undergo training in order to defend the new order. But the resources to train them, not only weapons but trained personnel at the right rank levels, were not so obviously available. Raúl had already established a series of schools for officers and other ranks of the armed forces and while these doubtless did indoctrinate them in revolutionary and indeed Marxist thought, they mostly tried to bring up the general level of education and culture in the force as a whole while giving it the most basic of military skills at the same time. The educational level of personnel has always been a problem for the FAR and in more limited ways continues to this day despite the massive efforts of the institution and the government as a whole.[26] Most of the leaders of the rebel force were not well educated and many came from the laboring classes and peasantry, which in Batista's Cuba could not possibly impress through their level of formal education or general knowledge. Many could hardly read and write. How to make training possible and effective under these circumstances was not obvious, especially if sophisticated weapons, equipment, and tactics were now to be put into place. And there was considerable reluctance to place old army cadres into teaching positions given their still untested loyalty to the new order.

Be that as it may, in the usual muddling through approach of the day, training and education did begin and thousands of young Cubans began to obtain the basics of military skills. While the lack of arms frustrated all, patience prevailed and progress was made. It was an interesting time for Raúl's own personal development in military skills, as well. If in Mexico he had gotten a reputation for adventure by wishing to learn, among other things, to be a *torero*, in the first months after victory he decided to take several further tactics and other military courses and even to learn to become a pilot.[27] The future air force Major-General Enrique Carreras was his flying instructor at the time and gives us some idea of what Raúl was like then and since:

> He was tireless, very young. I would have been 36 in those days, he a bit over 20. We began to get to know each other in the air and on the

ground. To tell the truth, I learned a lot from his example. Raúl is a
very capable chap, very well trained militarily, courageous and determined. He has helped the Revolutionary Armed Forces to become the
vanguard of the Revolution: Fidel has always confided in his direction,
organization and preparation.[28]

General José Ramón Fernández, another senior officer who knows
Raúl well, backs this view of the relationship:

Raúl is a revolutionary with great human qualities, very firm in his
principles, in the cause we defend, hard-working, organized, very systematic and disciplined. He is very demanding, especially of himself,
and then with others. We can say that if Fidel has been the founder of
the Rebel Army and the creator of its strategic concept, Raúl has been
the executor.[29]

It was also in these early months that the first internationalist adven-
tures of the new government were undertaken. Once again Raúl
found himself in the front line as minister in these. Fidel and he had
of course always been conscious of the need to work for what they saw
as the freedom of all Latin America and saw the Cuban Revolution as
part of something greater. And while Raúl lacked Fidel's important
and dramatic personal experience in the rest of the region, especially
in the massive upheaval of the *Bogotazo* in Colombia in 1948, he was
perfectly aware of the wider context.

Just before formally taking on the ministry, he explained what
the Revolution's approach would be where other efforts at national
or political liberation were concerned. While emphasizing that the
Revolution was not in the business of exporting itself, Raúl went on
to say, "It's that the revolutionary and transforming action of Cuba
breathes life into the Latin American peoples, gives them a higher con-
science of their strength, shows them that what they thought impossible, a thing of madmen and well-intentioned dreamers, is possible."
Thus while rejecting tyranny, he insisted, "It is not our job to change
governments or political and economic systems in other countries."
At the same time, he left no doubt about where Cuban sympathies lay
and left open how far Cuba might go in support of others.

We do not intervene in questions related to the national sovereignty of
other countries. But not intervening does not mean that we pretend
not to understand the struggle of those peoples, that we look with
indifference or wash our hands in the face of the inhuman crimes of

those retrograde, foreign, reactionary tyrannies, or that we are not going to give our solidarity, as a people.[30]

In fact, the Revolution was already helping out in a usually modest way a variety of Latin American antigovernment initiatives. And as the responsible minister for the armed forces, it was Raúl's job to provide this assistance. This could get carried away. In one early instance it appears that Fidel may not have been aware of the extent of Cuban assistance in a landing of dissidents in Panama and was embarrassed on his April trip to a variety of American capitals, including Washington, to find that such assistance had been made public. This may have led to one of the very few known disputes between the two brothers.[31]

Regarding helping dissidents in the Dominican Republic, however, the two could not have been in greater agreement. The Cubans, despite their difficulties with resources and lacking a structure to channel aid, went out of their way to assist in the expeditions mounted against the Trujillo regime in Santo Domingo in the first months of 1959. They went so far as to deploy some of the army's best units to the east, as well as naval ships to sea, in order to cover the June attempts to unseat the dictator. Raúl himself deployed to Oriente to oversee this support, which continued for years in one form or another after the abject failure of the 1959 efforts.[32] The need for arms was more than ever evident as Trujillo engaged Havana in a war of words that came close to becoming something more than that. And a new organization to support such attempts would also be needed. It was soon in place under Comandante Manuel Piñeiro Losada, known to all as Barba Roja; he was the eventual head of the Americas Department at the *Comité Central* (Central Committee of the Party) and, of course, also with time was to answer to Raúl.

The first part of the next year, February 1960, saw the opening of a Soviet commercial and technical exhibition in Havana, after which a bilateral commercial agreement was signed, and in March, there was the explosion of the French merchant ship *La Coubre* in Havana harbor, which ended all hope that the United States would avoid military action and violent sabotage and subversion to end the revolutionary experiment. In the second half of the year, following the unilateral abrogation of Cuban sugar quota arrangements by the United States, major nationalizations of US and other foreign property began. At the same time, the discovery of clandestine US bases that were training exiles to invade Cuba was made, and the *Comités de Defensa de la Revolución* (Committees of Defense of the Revolution), popular neighborhood groupings to search out counterrevolutionary activity as well as to provide social support for those in need, began to operate, although at a low level.

At the end of the year, the first shipments of arms arrived (artillery, small arms, and mortars) from the Soviet bloc, an event that followed the dispatch in May of 17 artillery officers to Czechoslovakia and others to China to undergo artillery training.[33] Raúl made a series of decisions as to how to modify demands on the militia at this time in order to hurt economic production as little as possible, since the call-up of militia personnel implied their leaving their normal place of work for both training and deployment. Each time there was an invasion scare, however, Raúl was obliged to stop what he was doing and dash off to Oriente, his battle position in case of war. The same occurred with other leaders, but Raúl had the farthest to go and arguably one of the most exposed places to defend.[34] The armed forces were divided into the three armies and territorial divisions, called at the time *Fuerzas de Combate Tácticas* (Tactical Combat Forces), they were to use to this day. All of this preparation was to be put to the test in short order.

The New Defense Structure Challenged: The Bay of Pigs

In April 1961, the Central Intelligence Agency (CIA) coordinated the first full-fledged military attempt to overthrow the Revolution to date. It launched Brigada 2506, a formation of largely Cuban exile personnel some 1,400 strong, onto the southern coast of Cuba in the remote area of the *Bahía de Cochinos* (Bay of Pigs) at Playa Girón, west of the major port city of Cienfuegos. The troops had been undergoing training by CIA and other US officials for some months in Central American bases. They were recruited, paid, and organized by the US government and initially it was intended that they were to receive powerful US military backing at the time of the invasion.[35]

Instead, that backing was reduced massively by the incoming administration of President John F. Kennedy, who had clear reservations about the wisdom of such action in the context of international and especially inter-American relations as they then stood. And while there was some very limited US military backing given, and even a few US casualties in direct support of the landing, the brigade was essentially left to its own devices to take on the Cuban armed forces and their new militia force.

Air raids on Cuba's air force bases preceded the invasion and led to the destruction of much of the small force the country could mount in its own air defense. But what remained vigorously attacked the landing zone and the ships that were unloading men and material. The brigade's personnel had been told that the Cuban population was just waiting for them in order to welcome them as liberators, and that the militia would desert to them in waves. Thus, the resistance in the air came as a shock; it would not be the last.

The still poorly trained and equipped militia, the local units completely without battle experience—although others had recently bested the counterrevolutionaries in the island's central mountains—met the invasion with determination if not professionalism. Far from surrendering or fleeing, they stood and delayed the invasion for key periods allowing Fidel, who at first thought the landings at Playa Girón to be merely a feint, to come down to the area and lead the fighting himself and to do so accompanied by more experienced regular troops.[36] At the same time, the new security apparatus and the Committees for the Defense of the Revolution arrested or at least detained thousands who might have stood by the invaders.

The attack fizzled miserably in the face of this determined resistance. Even the intended diversionary landing of 164 men in Oriente was a fiasco and did not even occur, as when the boats approached the shore they found Raúl's militia actively patrolling the area.[37] And on the central beach zones at Girón, chaos led to surrender after two days of sometimes fierce fighting. Almost the whole force was taken prisoner. But Cuba's revolution also had if not its first then certainly its most numerous group of martyrs. In 66 hours of battle, the FAR and its militias had taken over 350 casualties of whom 156 were killed in action.[38]

The armed forces, led by Fidel but organized and trained by Raúl, had stood the test and held their own. The Revolution trumpeted "imperialism's first defeat," and indeed the event was the first time in history that a determined military effort engineered or mounted officially by the United States to unseat an "undesirable" government in Latin America had failed. But also found were only too obvious problems with the defense organization of the country. It was courage and forcefulness more than organization that had won the day. A look at the rank levels of personnel coordinating the resistance shows that this was a young person's war and one with determination as the key factor in victory. For in the defensive operation, the officer responsible as chief of operations was a mere second lieutenant; of intelligence, a militia lieutenant; of communications, a corporal; of artillery and mortars, a militia lieutenant; and of weaponry, a captain.[39]

Fidel, however, was troubled by the very success of his defensive operation. For he was certain, as were most observers at the time, that the United States could not and would not accept such a reverse and that now it would be obliged to opt for more direct, regular military action to do away with the Cuban Revolution once and for all. Planning on the island took this as a given and the connection with the Soviet Union grew as Cuba asked for further military assistance and expanded both the size and level of training of its forces. By the end of 1961, the FAR could count on almost 100,000 more personnel, between regulars and reserves, than it could have a year-and-a-half before and could by then deploy 138,000 troops in defense of the island in case of attack.[40] It also had, from mid-1961, a centralized air defense system based on modern radar and antiaircraft weapons all of course obtained from the Soviet Union and its allies.

The October 1962 Missile Crisis found Raúl at the center of the drama. As had become usual, it was he who was sent to Moscow for the round of military talks that were to deepen cooperation in the spring of 1962. And it appears that it was at this meeting that the Soviets suggested that offensive missiles could be placed on the island in order to assist with the deterrence strategy the Cuban government had established. The Cubans were of course delighted that Moscow was willing to contemplate such a clear demonstration of their willingness to stand by the island in case of crisis. However, Cuban analysts insist that Fidel early on made clear that he assumed that such a deployment would be a public one and not secret, because he felt it would very likely be discovered by US intelligence and cause a crisis if the latter choice were taken. Indeed, much of the value of the deployment would come, in his view and given the deterrent role of the missiles, from its being known to the United States.[41]

His worst misgivings were to prove only too well founded. The Soviets did not agree and wished the deployment to be kept a secret. And when the Cubans worried out loud that this could easily bring on a serious crisis, the Soviets merely replied that Cuba need not be concerned, that in the worst case the Baltic Fleet could always be sent to the Caribbean to stand by the Cubans.[42] In August the first elements of the *Agrupación de Tropas Soviéticas* (Group of Soviet Troops or ATS) arrived.

Disaster was not long in coming. The United States discovered the deployment, denounced the Soviet Union in the United Nations for irresponsible adventurism, and "quarantined" the island with a major and effective naval blockade. For nearly two weeks the world stood as close as it has ever been to nuclear war as neither side would back down. Eventually Moscow not only did so but reached an agreement to dismantle the missile deployment over the heads of the Cuban government and its wishes that even if surrender was necessary, the crisis at least be used to make some progress on outstanding matters such as continued US control over the Guantánamo naval base.

None of this was to happen and Cuban-Soviet relations reached the lowest point they were to know until the early 1990s. Years of coldness were only overcome when Cuba's need for Soviet military and economic support became so strong that Havana was obliged to take steps to patch up the quarrel. When Che Guevara was killed in Bolivia in late 1967, it sounded the death knell for the "export of revolution" phase of Cuban foreign policy, always a thorn in the bilateral relationship with Moscow because of the latter's desire to not find itself embroiled in issues with Washington over what the Soviets felt were essentially minor or at least peripheral matters. At the same time, the Cuban economy was going through one of its worst moments.

In addition, on an issue of paramount importance to the Soviet Union where it found itself immensely isolated in the greater inter-national and even international communist arenas, Cuba backed Moscow on the question of the invasion of Czechoslovakia in 1968. Fidel went out of his way to find acceptable reasons as to why Moscow was obliged to act in this way and did so with the full prestige he had gained in the communist world and in the Non-Aligned Movement.[43] The Soviets could not have been more grateful, and the two countries were soon moving to a level of cooperation, including in the security and defense fields, that they had never known before.

In order to better understand the need for Soviet assistance, how-ever, it is important to turn to one more success the FAR and Raúl knew at this time, about which little has been written. Yet it was something so fierce, it led Raúl himself to call it *la segunda guerra civil* (the second civil war). This refers to the long and difficult strug-gle against what the Cuban government calls *bandidismo* (banditry), the usually but not always CIA-inspired resistance to the Revolution in the countryside in the 1960s. We have seen how there were nuclei of armed resistance to Fidel as early as mid-1959, centered essentially around opposition to the Reforma Agraria. But by no later than early 1960, the CIA had begun a major operation to recruit, inspire, train, pay, and supply such opposition in as many parts of the country as possible.

The spread of fighting was troubling indeed to the new government which was aware of the potential for trouble if such groups, especially in the key mountain range of the Escambray in central Cuba, could join with any attacking force coming in from abroad. Fidel and Raúl organized a first effort, termed *Operación Jaula* (Operation Cage), to deal with the challenge that could in no way be addressed by those internal security arrangements already in place, such as the *Departamento de Investigaciones del Ejército Rebelde* (Department of Investigations of the Rebel Army or DIER), the first such agency, set up as early as January 1959, working against subversion.[44] The success was exceptional and by the time of the Playa Girón landing in April 1961, the counterrevolution was disarticulated and completely unable to assist the invaders.

The longer struggle, however, lasted until 1965. The rebels operated in many parts of the country and kept the relatively small regular and militia organizations of the state busy indeed. Only slowly did they come under control, and their elimination was a manpower-intensive job that gave the militia good training but seriously depleted the resources of the state at the same time. Once again, the lack of weapons caused concern for the government, and the Soviet equipment left behind when the ATS was withdrawn in late 1963 was important in arming the militia forces without whom the regulars would have been hard-pressed to defeat the counterrevolutionaries.[45]

We can now return to the situation after Che's death and the 1968 events in Prague. The "Sovietization" of the FAR, a firm policy option only to be implemented formally as such in the early 1970s, could already be seen in some fashion beginning in earnest at this time with Soviet equipment, weapons, training, tactics, strategic concepts, drill, uniforms, intelligence techniques, educational approaches, and virtually everything else imaginable being brought into the Cuban forces. And while the official adoption of things Soviet was to wait another half-decade, the FAR was already being simply remade in the Soviet image with even that country's military ranks and many of its traditions later incorporated into the Cuban military. This is not to suggest that the FAR lost its *Cubania* (Cuban-ness) entirely, something that was an impossibility, but it is to say that this was doubtless the most complete adopting of a foreign military system by a Latin American army since the "Prussianization" of the Chilean Army in the late nineteenth century.

It is interesting to note, however, that in the crucial area of political control of the armed forces, Soviet practice was not followed. While political officers were attached to units of the FAR, they were under command of, and did not oversee, their own military unit commanding officers. The central idea of unity of command was retained and commanding officers wrote the annual military evaluations of their political officers and not the other way around. In addition, one's rank in the FAR determined one's rank in the party and not vice versa.[46] Fidel and Raúl had far too much military experience in wartime, and too much need to have effective armed forces, to allow for Soviet practice to apply here.

In weapons and equipment terms alone, the FAR went from being still very much US-based in what was in its arsenal to being almost entirely Soviet. The bulk of the total transfers of weaponry undertaken in the nearly 40 years of bilateral defense relations was staggering and, while the exact figures are not known, included several hundred main battle tanks, at least 30 light amphibious tanks, nearly 100 armored reconnaissance vehicles, almost 200 armored infantry fighting vehicles, several hundred armored personnel carriers, dozens of self-propelled artillery pieces, and nearly 200 of the famous Soviet multiple rocket launchers.[47]

While not having the FAR abandon revolutionary tasks such as participation in the Ten Million Ton *zafra* (sugar harvest) of 1970 or a wider role in agricultural production, or indeed the medical support role in the countryside, the desire of the Cuban government was to have as professional forces as possible and to have them as soon as this could be done. Raúl was to oversee this transformation, as well.

During the years of coolness between Moscow and Havana, the latter had been obliged to take defense even more seriously in some senses. While pleased to some degree that the agreement to end the Missile Crisis at least appeared to include an undertaking on the part of Washington not to invade the island, Cuba could not of course take such a thing at face value, and its official status was and is in question to this day. Given the Soviet Union's distance over these years, the decision had been taken to reinforce the deterrence posture of the country with a measure which historically would be difficult but which in the circumstances of the day it was felt the Cuban people would understand and accept.

Military service has never been popular in Cuba. And while it was at times compulsory under Spain and under the pseudo-republic, in the former it was only applied in wartime and in the latter it never was applied in a systematic fashion at all. It is admitted by Cuban officers who very much wish it were not so that Cubans do not take to military service happily.[48] They often make very good soldiers but they rarely wish to do so. However, the defense situation of the post–Missile Crisis island did not allow for any other option, and in 1963 compulsory military service for the relatively lengthy period of three years was introduced. And this time it was applied vigorously and to virtually all male youth upon reaching adulthood.

Cuba thus had, even in the difficult period of 1963 through 1968, a large manpower pool if not necessarily the best level of weaponry to arm it to show the United States that invasion would be costly if the apparent commitment not to invade was abandoned. And when Sovietization began in earnest again in the last years of the decade, it affected a huge number of young people now in uniform either in that larger regular FAR or in the even larger *milicias*.

The Other Security Services

At this point we should look at the other security services set up over these years. While it is the intention of this book to look essentially at Raúl's military life, the Cuban context is such that defense involves much more than strictly military activities. From early on in the new government, threats from abroad and at home abounded, as we have seen, and while preparation for deterrence and defense by the FAR could deal with some, it could not manage all.

A main threat was to the life of the comandante en jefe himself. In the Sierra, this could be addressed as part of the military defense of the rebel forces. But in government, it would have to be done differently. We have seen that early on the DIER was set up in part to provide personal security for the *líder máximo* (maximum leader), but it also served to provide such services to the leadership more generally. Soon it could be said that if Cuba was threatened, the regime was even more so and the head of that regime more so still. And Raúl and other comandantes, especially Che Guevara, were also considered for assassination by the CIA since it was felt by some that only by taking out all three could one ensure the regime collapse so desired by Washington.[49]

The events before and around the Bay of Pigs invasion gave the green light for the development of a much more sophisticated and revolutionary range of security services than had been seen in probably any Latin American government to date. Fidel could now more than justify the deployment of major resources to an internal and external threat that had finally shown its teeth publicly. No one could now doubt that the United States would stop at virtually nothing to overthrow the new government. As the US-orchestrated diplomatic and economic isolation of Cuba gained pace, and terror, sabotage, infiltration, suborning of personnel, and the like became as of March 1960 the standard instruments of US policy in dealing with Castro, the latter moved forcefully to counter this wide range of threats, giving of course Raúl the overseeing of this task, as well.[50]

At first the effort was largely homegrown. The CDRs and the *Brigadas de Producción y Defensa* (Production and Defense Brigades) were the first mass organizations for internal control placed outside the FAR military reserve system, although there had been some smaller groupings put into place earlier on. The first of the CDRs were more visible than the second and were begun even before the US attack, in September 1960, in order to discover and denounce counterrevolutionary activity at home. Comandante Ramiro Valdés was named to head the *Organos de Seguridad del Estado* (State Security Organs) and there was to be over time a CDR cell in each block of the cities, and every hamlet of the countryside, the length and breadth of the island. As we have partially seen, it was their work that was largely responsible for the effective neutralizing of potential support for the 1961 landing through the arrest or temporary detention of some twenty thousand people during the invasion attempt.[51] Their local knowledge was also helpful in the actual area of the beaches where the landings took place, and they were of great use there in providing first aid and medicine, in preparing food, transporting weapons, and other tasks on the spot.

This demonstration of the potential value of such a local popular organization was not lost on the Castro brothers, who were determined to expand the CDRs. The eight thousand branches were to grow to a hundred thousand and the total number of members from a hundred thousand to about one million for 1962. These *cederistas* (CDR personnel) were rarely full-time workers but rather volunteers at block or village level who took turns working against counter-revolutionary activities. However, with their growing size and capabilities, they were soon given new tasks such as recuperating natural resources, assisting with the provision of medical care, organizing Che's little-loved and mightily criticized system of *trabajo voluntario* (voluntary labor), providing support for those called up for military service, and assisting with revolutionary propaganda and instruction. They were often also called upon to help with education, sports, and cultural tasks at local levels.[52]

Under the highly difficult conditions of the Special Period, they later became involved in even wider fields such as conducting the census of edible fats, recuperating valuables and vaccination campaigns, updating the electoral register and making up the list of electors, providing local support at the poll booths and personnel for electoral commissions at their various levels, organizing blood banks, helping with the frequent political mobilizations so characteristic of Fidel's style of government, and fighting common delinquency.[53] At the same time, they expanded their role in the distribution of food and medicine to the elderly, personal visits to the homes of the infirm, and other greatly valued social roles of this type which generally are much appreciated by Cuban society at large.

That same period, however, saw the decline of the efficiency of the CDRs in some of their roles because of the strains it implied for all. It is difficult to have a vigilance system functioning normally if, as the Cuban 1990s saying has it, *aquí todos somos ilegales* (here we are all illegal). That is, in the Cuba of the Special Period virtually everyone had to be in some sort of illegal activity to get by since official salaries and the *libreta* (ration card) were not enough for a normal family to manage in a decent fashion. Thus one could not easily denounce law breakers when one was in a similar situation oneself.

The CDRs remain nonetheless a valuable arm of the state, one that reaches down into every neighborhood of the nation however rural and seemingly unimportant and keeps the state advised on local conditions and attempts to help keep those conditions under control. And the fact that they report up the chain of command to the Minister of the Armed Forces and are more recently part of the *Sistema Unico de Vigilancia* (Unified System of Vigilance), put in place to face the trials of the Special Period in the early 1990s, means that the FAR have a direct connection with internal security at the top of the state structure even when it does not wish any such role lower down.[54]

The Brigadas de Producción y Defensa are less important, although they can come to life to defend the Revolution in style as was seen in their role in frustrating the *Habanazo* rioting of August 2004.[55] The brigadas are trade unions or other mass organizations, locally based groups of workers or farmers who, within their factory or agricultural operation, agree to mobilize in support of the Revolution if threatened and to do good work in general if called upon to do so in any tasks they might be given. They are not in any sense as pervasive as the CDRs but do also report up the chain through MINFAR at the top.

In addition to the CDRs and brigadas and at the top of the wide series of institutions dealing with the safety of the Revolution is *Seguridad del Estado* (State Security), a body responsible with MININT directly for internal security matters. Headed in the early years by the highly trusted close collaborator of Raúl's Comandante, Ramiro Valdés, in 1985 it passed to General José Abrantes Fernández who headed it and then MININT as a whole until the Ochoa Affair four years later. The elements of this system are not widely known, but they include those responsible for Fidel's personal security as well as that of Raúl and certain other key figures.[56]

Late in the key year of 1961, the *Dirección General de Inteligencia* (Directorate General of Intelligence) was set up as the principle state intelligence agency which it remains to this day. It tackled and still deals with intelligence collection and analysis as well as spearheading the "export of revolution" phase of Cuban foreign policy to which reference has already been made. Early on organized along Soviet lines, it has three operational elements: political and economic, external counterintelligence, and military intelligence.[57] There are thought to be many overlaps between the various intelligence agencies, and there is resulting disagreement about their overall efficiency. The US intelligence expert Brian Latell, who watches the island closely although only from abroad, calls the Cuban intelligence and security apparatus one of the five or six best in the world while Mexico's ambassador to Cuba in the early 2000s, Richard Pascoe Pierce, who dealt closely with various branches of it over two important years, 2001 and 2002, has a different reading of their quality and believes they are, largely because of overlapping jurisdictions, not as good as reported.[58] It is clear that despite these interpretations of MININT and in general Cuban intelligence and security, they can only be considered good at their job since no senior leader of the *cúpula* (the cupola or highest levels of command in the state) has ever been assassinated, despite so many attempts, and the regime is still there.

MININT is a vast ministry with responsibility for a very wide range of internal and even some external elements of national defense. It is in charge of everything from the customs service to the fire brigade, from the coast guard to immigration. It is omnipresent and even has its own special forces which do have a role in suppressing disorder if it raises its head.[59] As mentioned elsewhere, the FAR is quite pleased to be able to distance itself from such roles, which so dramatically offer the possibility of having to abandon the constant theme of a revolutionary force like theirs of *el ejército no tira contra el pueblo* (the army does not fire on the people). And MININT allows them to do just this. But it is important not to be too credulous here. Especially since the Ochoa Affair in 1989, MININT in many senses belongs to MINFAR and is at the highest levels often officered by FAR personnel.

Thus while it is true that the FAR does not do internal security training as most armies in one form or another do or have done, the ministry does in a variety of important ways indirectly oversee another security force, which most definitely does have that role and priority. And if in the peaceful days of the early twenty-first century internal security problems may seem far away, a fact underscored by the absolutely peaceful succession in the presidency of 2006 through 2008, it is not that long ago that they seemed anything but distant. It is interesting to note that the major defense exercise of 2009 took a successful US attempt to destabilize the government as an excuse for military intervention, to be its scenario for the practice exercise. It is also worth keeping in mind that all previous invasions of Cuba by the United States, including the one that took place as part of the war with Spain in 1898, were explained to the US public and world public opinion not as invasions, but as humanitarian operations to restore order.[60] Indeed, even the current US Southern Command or Southcom (the US military command responsible for most of Latin America) has very recently used such a scenario in its own contingency planning and exercises related to Cuban events.

The 1970s

After the disaster of the failed sugar zafra of 1970, the FAR settled into a major program aimed at becoming more professional. There was widespread recognition that the deployment of so much in the way of military resources and time to not strictly military objectives had damaged the vital drive for a more professional armed force able to continue to deter attack. Sovietization, which became paramount with the decision in 1971 to adopt Soviet structures and organization in the FAR, required a great deal in the way of settling into new procedures, and there was much training and education required to bring the still inadequate force up to standard.[61] Hundreds and finally thousands of officers, NCOs, and technicians went to the Soviet Union and other Warsaw Pact countries to train. Many thousands more were trained by Soviet instructors on the island, although where possible the Cuban preference was for the Soviets to "train the trainers," letting Cubans have the direct contact with the rank-and-file soldiery. Nonetheless, a strong connection between the Soviets and the Cubans was established, and while the official link was often strained, on a personal basis many friendships were established and many personnel even intermarried.[62]

Raúl ensured that the relationship remained profitable to Cuba and that the FAR remained anything but a political tool of the Soviets, while also seeing occasions, such as the deployments to Africa later in the decade, where mutual advantage could be obtained from closely working together. Fidel's unique and firm negotiating techniques appear to have done the rest.[63]

The revolutionary credentials of the FAR might well have been thought to be shifting downward with all this professionalization, but this potential trend was not allowed to develop. In the first place, the economy continued to need FAR support especially in the agricultural manpower field. Indeed, it was in 1973 that the FAR founded the *Ejército Juvenil de Trabajo* (Youth Labor Army or EJT), essentially an agricultural labor force in uniform that was used, while its members were doing their compulsory service, to farm and harvest. Reaching some hundred thousand personnel, it has done sterling service to the state, particularly after Cuba was hit by the Special Period in the 1990s.[64]

In other fields, however, the FAR also retained revolutionary roles at home and got new ones abroad as the 1970s progressed. While its support for the national effort to assist "progressive" forces in Latin America had slowed dramatically as of the death of Che, it had not ended entirely and was rekindling in support of leftist movements in Central America in that decade. At home, it was still engaged in everything from blood donor clinics to natural disaster preparation and recovery.

From 1962 and for a decade, the FAR assisted with the sugar harvest. Indeed, Raúl boasted in 1973 that even without the EJT, the FAR had "cut 5,583 million *arrobas* of cane between 1965 and 1973."[65] And he expressed his confidence that in the future, with the EJT in place, that figure would be much higher.

Many schools received their basic sanitary assistance from the armed forces from 1973 until 1980 and the fight against dengue fever was in part a FAR responsibility from the end of the 1970s on.[66] The armed forces continued to be seen in almost all walks of life, helping the public face its challenges. And while it must be said that many other armed forces in Latin America have development or rural medical responsibilities, in Cuba those roles had become vastly more complicated, sophisticated, and ubiquitous than in any other country in the region.

If it was radical to deploy armed forces over such a huge range of national activities at home, it was abroad that the Cuban military was to become best known in the 1970s. While insurrection may have petered out in most of Latin America by those years, this was not the case in Africa, especially in Portuguese colonial Africa. Cuba had already sent limited assistance to Algeria in its stand-off with Morocco in the early 1960s and was to help even Syria in organizing its defenses a decade later. But it was in southern Africa and then in the Horn that Cuba acted most decisively and with greatest effect.

Fidel has often described this assistance as part of Cuba's outstanding debt to Africa, resulting from the monstrous and massive importation of millions of black slaves from the sixteenth to the nineteenth century. Be that as it may, the Cuban effort was, for a country of its size, truly massive—a commitment over many years first to the defeat of Portugal and the liberation of its colonies and then in the struggle with South Africa over Angola and Namibia's future and in the wars in the Horn of Africa.[67] Incredibly, over three hundred thousand Cuban soldiers fought in Africa and two thousand lost their lives there. This is by far the largest overseas military engagement and series of operations conducted by a Latin American country in the history of the region and completely outstrips even the efforts of Brazil in World War II.[68] And it was conducted by a country with less than ten million people.

These conflicts marked the FAR and Cuba to this day, with many people wondering why the country engaged in them at all and others feeling that the endeavors constitute what was essentially Cuba's finest hour. From a strictly military point of view, however, it is impossible to deny the positive impacts of the deployments. The armed forces met a very good Western-style army and air force and did very well indeed against them. The South Africans who fought the Cubans in southern Africa are nearly unanimous in their praise for the FAR in terms of its fighting capacity. Cubans showed their ability to engage a serious enemy over long periods of time, with exceptional logistics challenges in play, and to do so successfully. The FAR gained innumerable combat veterans who still provide the army and air force with special advantages in knowledge of what all armed forces view as the "real thing,"—that is, combat in earnest with a proper enemy. And if the experience in the Horn, where the FAR instructed and fought alongside Ethiopians during the Somali invasion of 1977/8, was neither as impressive nor as successful politically, it showed what the Cubans could do and brought back to the island the kind of military experience at the harder end of the spectrum of conflict that all armed forces should ideally try to prepare for professionally.[69]

Thus at the end of two decades as minister, Raúl could look back on exceptional success. He had the second largest, numerically speaking, armed forces in Latin America ready to defend the country. He had as well a functioning level of cooperation with the lesser of the two superpowers, which was nonetheless a country of great weight militarily. And he had a well-trained, combat experienced, and well-armed military, and an army with revolutionary credentials second to none in the world.[70]

The FAR had shown itself capable of supporting and training revolutionaries in other countries, of themselves fighting serious enemies and winning far from the island's shores, of being more than able to be a major element in the deterrence of any thought of attacking Cuba on the part of the United States, and of being active in producing a reserve force unheard of in size, training, equipment, and speed of mobilization anywhere in the region, as well as being a loyal and flexible tool supportive of the revolutionary government's goals at home and abroad. And the FAR, through Cuba's unique position in both the socialist world and the Non-Aligned Movement, enjoyed an intelligence access situation absolutely unheard of even in the most developed nations. Its prestige soared especially in the Third World but also at home.

Raul could well be proud of what he had, with Fidel's inspiration, achieved. And if Fidel's well known keenness to run military things himself had once again shown itself in the Angolan fighting, no one doubted that it was Raul who kept things on the rails and made the day to day efficiency of the FAR what it was. Indeed, even there, where Fidel, albeit from far away Havana, took a huge interest in the way the war was conducted, it was the minister himself who went to the country and was in the field helping set up the arrangements under which the Cubans would fight. Fidel certainly took a key role when things were tough on the ground in that far-off campaign, but Raul was the man managing things across the board and with the comandante en jefe's full confidence.

Chapter 3

More Thinking Required: The 1980s and the Weakening of the Soviet Connection

The 1980s were to prove to be years of considerable challenge for the institution that the FAR had become and indeed for revolutionary Cuba as a whole. These challenges were to involve both economic and security issues and, as in the past, the FAR was not to see its role restricted to the latter. The Cuban economy continued to have grave difficulties in finding its feet under the variety of experiments with the implementation of socialism upon which the government embarked. And despite very favorable terms for the island in the socialist division of labor to which it quite fully belonged after joining the Eastern Bloc's *Consejo de Ayuda Mutua Económica* (Comecon, the Council for Mutual Economic Assistance or CAME) in 1972 but whose members had been its chief commercial partners since 1961, the Cuban economy retained many problems of importance.[1] By the middle of the decade, it became necessary to embark on a program of *rectificación* (rectification) in an effort to overcome the main difficulties encountered. In some ways, however, this was a minor inconvenience when compared to the problems occasioned by the arrival of Ronald Reagan in the White House as of January 1981.

The "Rollback" of Communism

The presidential election campaign in the United States in the autumn of 1980 was in many respects based on how to beat the communist challenge, which was perceived in that country as its central foreign policy objective in the Cold War years. Defeat in Vietnam in the early

1970s had shaken US confidence in its leadership and military capabilities, and during President Jimmy Carter's years in office he had, at least initially, sought methods other than direct confrontation as ways to deal with Moscow and the international communist movement. In this context, relations with Cuba were reopened although not at a full diplomatic level, and *Oficinas de Intereses* (Interest Sections) were established in both of the respective capitals. Exchanges in cultural, travel, educational, and some other fields were also undertaken.[2]

Under increasing fire from the right in the lead-up to the election campaign, however, President Carter froze some of these initiatives and attempted to show that he also could not be called "soft on communism" because of his opening up to the Cubans. And with the decline in the relationship brought on by Cuban operations in southern Africa, the progress that had been made was all but forgotten.

President Ronald Reagan was quite another man. His visceral anticommunist stance was well-known, and his campaign included repeated promises to "roll back" communism after the defeats the United States had suffered in recent years. At least publicly, he felt the only way to deal with the Soviet Union was to drive it into ferocious economic and military confrontation, which would lead inevitably to its defeat and US victory in the Cold War. His premise was that the Soviet Union could not sustain real competition from the West and that all that was necessary to show that weakness for all to see was to sufficiently increase the pressure.

In Reagan's view, Cuba stood out as a particular thorn in the side of the United States. He repeatedly referred to it as a "vassal state" of the USSR and called for "immediate action" of a "punitive" kind against it and publicly told the island's government that it would be obliged to pay a "high price" for its support of the Soviets.

In this context the Soviets, who well knew that elements of the Reagan analysis were true where their own staying power economically and militarily were concerned, were soon to let Havana know where they stood. In a direct reply to a question from Raúl, the man who perhaps knew them best after himself making so many defense deals with them, the Soviets told him that in case of military or even serious diplomatic confrontation with the United States, Cuba would be on its own and the USSR's support would be limited to the moral field.[3] And while Cuba had not been expecting huge Soviet assistance in case of a serious worsening of the dispute with the United States, it had expected that the most likely conflict scenarios would find Moscow and Havana in it together at least to some degree. Thus, this new stance was a major blow.

Fidel and Raúl set to work to find means to address this new challenge—a president of the United States determined to defeat communism around the world and a Soviet Union equally determined to give him no excuse for adventurism at its expense. Moscow was to be sent reeling in the Middle East, to some degree in Central America, and in many other parts of the world over the decade and found itself hard pressed indeed to keep up with the US economic and military surge under Reagan. Under all three of its last leaders—Andropov, Chernenko, and later Gorbachev—it was to have no intention of becoming embroiled again over any issue as peripheral to its survival as Cuba.

The result was the most important program of reform for the armed forces that Cuba had experienced since the mid-1960s. While in no way jettisoning Soviet assistance or much of the model provided in many spheres by the Soviet armed forces, the Cuban leadership began to search for ways to ensure that its longstanding deterrence posture still held up despite the obvious lack of anything like a Soviet "alliance."

In this context, it was not the USSR or China that offered Cuba the most useful model but rather the recently victorious Vietnamese armed forces which had not only sustained a decades-long struggle with the French and then the United States but had also ended up with absolute victory and the reunification of the country under communist leadership. General Vo Nguyen Giap became compulsory reading for Cuban officers with his *People's War, People's Army* seemingly giving a guide as to how a determined people could overcome apparently impossible odds.[4]

Fidel, Cuban sources agree, once again was to have the idea for how to react and Raúl the responsibility to make that idea reality.[5] In May 1980, Fidel announced in the Plaza de la Revolución in Havana that there was to be a return to the nation in arms idea and that more arms production would henceforth be done at home with a consequent lessening of dependence on the Soviets. Thus was born the Cuban version of *Guerra de Todo el Pueblo* (War of All the People), a concept not as far from traditional Cuban deterrence thinking as some would have it, but one that nonetheless had many new elements to it and one Raúl had been working on for some months as relations with the United States worsened in the last period of the Carter presidency

Raúl had as usual commissioned serious studies of the situation and the prospects for new approaches to the evolving context and himself explained the leadership's thinking on the subject at Santiago in that first year of the Reagan presidency and in the presence of new units of the FAR resulting from the new strategic posture. He asserted, "The masses have understood that the new United States administration represents a clear danger and are preparing to confront it" and that the idea would be to create a " powerful reserve capable of multiple combat missions, as well as others related to the safety and defense of factories and installations, bridges, railroads, access routes, and to participate in the engineering works to prepare the ground to contribute to the solution of innumerable problems that result from the struggle." Nor would the future reserve forces be made up entirely of personnel in the best physical condition. Instead, the requirement to have enormous numbers of people resisting invasion meant that use would be made of the "vast number of persons who do not enjoy the physical condition to submit to (full military) training...but who can cooperate in a multitude of tasks."[6] The idea would be to force the United States to face such a quantity of troops and combat capabilities that it would be impossible for it to contemplate aggression.

This was the key to the new thinking. Without any Soviet assurances at all, Cuba would face Washington with a strategic requirement of such proportions that if the United States chose to attack the island it would have no real chance of a quick victory and would have to contemplate a long and bloody struggle on its own doorstep. Essentially the newly organized *Tropas de Milicias Territoriales* (Territorial Militia Troops or MTT), alongside the regular force, the other militia and reserve formations, the Brigades of Defense and Production, and even the CDRs, would provide a force of such size that attack would be much more costly than any possible political advantage that might accrue from it. The nation in arms would become a reality and not a slogan with the MTT being made mobile, independent, dispersed, and specialized in antitank operations. The regular force would meet the first attack coming from the United States and other bases; would blunt that attack with professional naval, air, and land resources; and would then withdraw behind the shield of the reserves and MTT to begin preparing the long-range popular defense of the island using all its potential resources.

The result of these changes was the formation, with the new MTT battalions, of a force of some 800,000 men and women which, with the regular force of some 250,000, meant that Cuba disposed of a total of perhaps a million personnel who were or could be armed in order to effect a credible defense and resulting deterrence approach. In addition, for internal defense the CDRs were reinforced in numbers and effectiveness, and integrated into a new system of "Vigilancia-

FAR-CDR" that aimed at closer cooperation among the three elements of the internal security system of the country and gave new roles to the CDRs in connection with both the compulsory military service system and the militias.[7]

Continued supplies of Soviet weaponry were necessary to establish the force, and they kept coming despite, or perhaps in part because of, the Soviets feeling rather guilty about leaving the Cubans alone to face the United States at this crucial time. Cuba was thus able to not only continue with the expansion of its own forces but also to still help others. When the *Ejército Sandinista de Liberación Nacional* (Sandinista Army for National Liberation, or ESLN) took Managua in mid-1979 and established a leftist government there, the FAR was soon present to assist in its defense preparations against US direct attack or that country's support for the *contras,* the armed opposition that quickly developed to Sandinista rule. Despite what some analysts have asserted, the Cubans knew that the contras were often brave soldiers and that the ESLN required new strategies and tough, small, and mobile units to defeat them.[8] The Cuban government was clearly very determined to support its new friend in spite of the vast dangers of such a forward policy in the strategic context of the early to mid-1980s.

Attempts to do something similar in Grenada ended in abject failure, however, in October 1983 when a US invasion of the island not only unseated a leftist government there but also caused the death of 13 Cubans who died in the fighting. Given the US role in the Central American civil wars then occurring, the rollback of communism seemed only too real and the new preparations undertaken by Cuba had a backdrop easily explaining the need for them. Cuba was humiliated by the setback and not happy with the conduct of the commander on the ground in Grenada, but the FAR weathered this storm as well if not without difficulty and Raúl could welcome the bodies of the 13 back to Cuba emphasizing the clear need for a reinforced deterrence strategy in the current context. And after five years of MTT and other reforms related to the GTP, Raúl was able to say that an enemy invasion would find in Cuba not only a FAR with "a heightened level of mechanization, great firepower and a high maneuver capacity" but, in a wider sense, also a nation offering any enemy "*un gigantesco avispero popular*" (a gigantic wasp nest). As always, he continued to insist that "avoiding war is the equivalent of winning it," the bedrock of Cuban deterrence in national strategic thought.[9]

In 1986, a major exercise, *Bastión* 1986, was held to test command structures in complex situations and evaluate the evolving Cuban military art that Raúl had called for in the wake of the weakening of the Soviet connection. It was to be a *pensamiento militar fresco, ágil, e independiente* (fresh, agile, and independent military thought), and it certainly appeared to be all of that.[10]

As we have seen, however, the international context was not the only worry Havana had. The economy's performance was slipping badly as the 1980s wore on, and Fidel was determined to address the problem. In this context, Raúl brought up the possibility that some elements of military management might be tried in some industries as a sort of trial balloon to see if they could be made to improve things. Especially worrying were slack approaches to work, lack of discipline in the workplace, absenteeism on a large scale, black market practices, and related issues.

The *rectificación* (rectification) process included many elements of hoped-for improvements, but for the military industries the hope was for bettering range, flexibility, and efficiency. Fidel was losing confidence in the old Soviet-style *Sistema de Dirección y Planificación de la Economía* (Direction and Planning System of the Economy), and as early as 1984, Raúl was allowed to move forward with his own radical ideas for selected industries. Domingo Amuchástegui and Brian Latell have shown how Raúl hoped to improve things through the promotion of greater self-sufficiency in the FAR and a reduction of its dependence on the USSR, an increase in efficiency and productivity in military factories (*Unión de Industrias Militares* or Union of Military Industries), and perhaps most importantly, the provision of a model for other parts of the economy to study and in certain circumstances apply.[11]

On April 19, 1986, Fidel denounced *el economicismo, el burocratismo, los egoismos y la corrupción* (economicism, bureaucratism, egoisms, and corruption) and formally began a process of *rectificación de errores y tendencias negativas* (rectification of errors and negative tendencies) and the application of Raúl's techniques of discipline, rewards for work done, and modern "management by results" techniques to a number of other state industries. In the Third Party Congress Raúl's approach was recognized by a call to address inefficiency and absenteeism with military discipline and a military sense of urgency and commitment.[12] A number of armed forces officers were sent to study business administration with some going abroad to Europe and Latin America to do so. And Raúl became interested in a closer look at the Chinese system of armed forces involvement in the economy, as well.

Whatever the impact of these changes more widely, Raúl's FAR had once again proven a fertile source for new ideas and practices and shown the way to improvements far removed from a traditional Latin American military mold. It was to stand the FAR, and Cuba, in good stead when things went from bad to much worse a few years later.

Few observers imagined the changes that were to come Cuba's way as a result of events in Eastern Europe as the decade ended. While Gorbachev's reforms in the Soviet Union had been blasted by Fidel as dangerous and sinister, the speed of events and their utterly uncontrollable nature surprised all. The collapse of communism in Eastern Europe shook Cuba but so did the savage repression in Tiananmen Square. The FAR, raised as we have seen quite sincerely on a daily diet of *este ejército no tira contra el pueblo*, found both events deeply disturbing. It was inconceivable to them that the armed forces of Eastern Europe would do absolutely nothing to defend their own ideology and governments to which they had sworn loyalty, and conversely that those of China would stop at absolutely nothing to do the same. The FAR could not contemplate either option. And if, as it turned out, they were not to be required to make that choice, they were to enter what can arguably be considered the period of greatest challenge they had ever faced. Fortunately for them, their leadership remained in the hands of Fidel and Raúl, in whom they clearly still had trust. And original ideas for survival were plentiful and in the end successful. But it was a near-run situation and in the early years of crisis that end was far from certain.

Indeed, before difficulties began in earnest, Cuba was shaken by its greatest scandal in many years. In circumstances that may never become entirely clear, a very senior officer of the FAR, General Arnaldo Ochoa Sánchez, who was highly decorated and even had the status of Hero of the Republic of Cuba, was found guilty of treason and shot, as were two other senior officers of the Ministry of the Interior. Ochoa had served as commander of the operation in Angola, had been the senior Cuban adviser with the ESLN in Nicaragua, and was an immensely popular officer enjoying the total confidence of not only Raúl but also of Fidel himself. The trial itself was a sensation and observers vied with each other for a *thèse de complot* that would explain the extraordinary events.

In the view of this author, attempts to be reductionist and find only one cause for the denouement of the Ochoa Affair are unlikely to get one very far in understanding it. Fidel was accused of stage-managing the trial and the events leading up to it and of simply framing Ochoa because the defendant was so popular that he stood as a possible successor to the líder máximo or even a replacement for him before he even decided to retire. Others suggested that Ochoa headed a group of pro-Gorbachev, pro-perestroika, and pro-glasnost senior officers within the FAR who were itching for power and wished to take Cuba on the reform route the USSR had chosen. Still others accepted uncritically that Ochoa had become an unwilling but incredibly naïve servant of Colombian *narcotraficantes* and simply did not understand the very serious possible consequences for Cuba of this sort of action by an officer of his seniority and in his position.

It seems more likely that all of the above played some role but the first two rather less than the last. There is little doubt that Ochoa had some sympathy for the Gorbachev program. Equally, there is no doubt that he was a popular officer with something of a following in military circles. But to move from there to suggest that he was in any real sense a possible replacement for Fidel is truly a leap of the imagination. Fidel Castro is Fidel Castro and no senior officer in the FAR, not even a hero such as Ochoa, could imagine himself stepping into Fidel's shoes, especially without Fidel's blessing for the proposed approach to the future. In the indictments of the general, there is not a hint of political activities the state had difficulty with, and despite the sensationalist rumors that abounded in Cuba and outside it at the time, there is no reason to think that there was a wider plot afoot at all.[13]

Instead, it was the lack of understanding of the potential damage to the Cuban state, and to Raúl in particular, that dealing with narcotraficantes could bring that made Ochoa's actions unacceptable and made Fidel and Raúl feel that an example had to be made of him. In 1987, the United States had declared the drug trade to be the country's main security and defense threat. In the declining years of the Cold War, and under the impact of closer relations with the Soviets, it seemed obvious enough that the USSR could not be considered such a threat any longer. But the impact of drugs on the US population certainly could be, and if President Nixon, as far back as the 1970s, "declared war" on drugs, Reagan went further still; he placed it as the era's main security challenge to the United States and moved forward to give the nation's armed forces a role in combating it.

In addition, doubtless for internal political purposes, the United States made determined attempts over this time to implicate Cuba, the Cuban armed forces, and Raúl himself as minister in the use of drugs to do damage to United States society through their role in the international drugs trade.[14] Such was the punch of these allegations that Cuba produced its first major rebuttal of these accusations that year, entitled "Cuba against the Drugs Trade," insisting that it had fiercely opposed both production and trade in the substances since the first rebel government in Cuba Libre (the territory in the Sierra Maestra and later in the Sierra Cristal that had been cleared of Batista's army) set about destroying such crops in 1957.[15]

Ochoa argued that because of the US embargo he had been using drugs as a means of obtaining money to purchase needed goods with hard currency and that none of that money had ever been kept by him or his associates. Fidel has accepted that this was the case, and the accusations against him did not include his own making of money in an illicit fashion.[16] But his connections with narcotraficantes, and his sending of serving officers to have contact with them—even with Pablo Escobar himself on at least one occasion—sealed his doom. Such contacts could be and were used by the United States to blacken the name of the revolutionary government and to prepare indictments in US courts against, among others, Raúl. Indeed, it appears that US federal agents were already on to Ochoa and his partners' trail by 1987 and that for more than just Washington there was a good deal of truth to the rumor of senior-level Cuban cooperation with drug running into the United States, cooperation for which in the end the minister of defense could be deemed responsible.[17]

Raúl was personally shocked by these events and the revelation of sustained irresponsibility that they reflected from a very senior officer who had long ago gained his confidence.[18] Fidel has gone to great lengths to show that there was no option but to use the maximum penalty in this case as the situation was so fraught with difficulties at the international level; it was vital to clear up things with a dramatic move that would capture the headlines worldwide. A major purge of MININT followed the trial, and the execution of the three officials and its repercussions are in some senses still felt.

A hint of worse things to come arrived only one month after Ochoa's indictment. At the annual July 26th commemoration ceremonies in 1989, Fidel told the crowd ominously, "We can no longer say with certainty if socialist camp supplies, which arrived with the precision of a clock for thirty years, will continue."[19] Within only a few months, that concern became reality as events in Eastern Europe led to the demise of socialist government across the region, and with that the annulling of the Warsaw Pact as well as COMECON and the beginning of the end for the Soviet Union itself. The impact on Cuba was gigantic and is still seen to this day.

Chapter 4

The Special Period for Raúl, the FAR, and Cuba

In July 1990, Fidel announced in even more dramatic fashion than usual that there would now be a modification of the standing national defense plan for time of war, termed a "special period"; it would now apply instead, with obviously major modifications, in time of peace. The end of the vast majority of Soviet trade with the island, and of all development cooperation, investment, and credit arrangements had come as a hammer blow and the comandante en jefe made no secret about the implications being a major period of belt-tightening such as revolutionary Cuba had never known before.

The shock was enormous. The economy was to shrink by a frightening 35 to 50 percent between 1989 and 1993. Exports suffered tremendously since before the disaster the Soviet Union had been taking 63 percent of Cuba's sugar (the country's main export), 73 percent of its nickel, 95 percent of its citrus, and 100 percent of its electrical components. And even imports were hard hit since the USSR had previously provided 63 percent of Cuban food imports, 80 percent of its imported machinery and equipment, 98 percent of what the country used for fuel, and 74 percent of other imported manufactured goods. In short, Cuba, a small dependent economy deeply tied into international trade, lost 80 percent of its purchasing power abroad over an extraordinarily short period.[1]

As if the above were not enough, initial calls for magnanimity on the part of the United States in regard to Cuba were quickly silenced, and a policy of bringing the country even more forcibly to its knees quickly gained acceptance. In 1992, the Torricelli Act passed Congress and greatly deepened what Cubans call *el bloqueo* (the blockade) and the US calls merely an embargo, making it even more difficult for Cuba to trade with other countries.

The emergency, as almost always, found the armed forces at the center of the national response. Raúl was clearly and constantly consulted as to how to move forward in the face of the disaster, although in the usual supportive role to the determining one played by Fidel. The country was reeling and soon hunger and illness were spreading in the very Latin American country where those problems had been most successfully addressed over many years. The main achievements of the Revolution were very hard hit indeed.

The FAR was directed to assist massively in dealing with the crisis. Raúl was told that from now on the military would have to feed itself and help feed the nation, that they would have to take an even greater role in earning foreign exchange for the state, and that they would have to be ready to help keep order in cooperation with MININT. In addition, they would need to be inventive in finding ways to reduce friction with the United States and demonstrate special attention to roles that Washington found helpful, such as antinarcotics operations to counter the narcotics trade and those dealing with the control of illegal migration. The FAR would need to be more flexible than ever to answer the needs of the nation without losing its ability to deter attack, which was perhaps now more possible than ever before.

The problem, not surprisingly, was that the FAR was itself also hard hit by the crisis. The loss of some 14 million tons of fuel annually struck the forces in a particularly strong way, dependent as they were on those imports for training and operations. Raúl immediately called a meeting for the principal leaders of the government where he encouraged criticism and self-criticism and where he gave his own views on concrete elements that needed rectification or modification. He expected the FAR to be the first in making those changes and it moved quickly to do so. Soon the forces were nearly self-sufficient in agricultural production, except for a few commodities, to the extent of some 80 to 90 percent of their consumption.[2] Other areas were harder to deal with. Fuel and other strategic reserves, held as sacred by both Raúl and Fidel, were greatly depleted in an attempt to salvage the economy, although it appears that food and essential materials stocks, for example those for natural disasters, did not suffer the same fate. In the area of fuel available, the forces had some units at 30 percent of what had become standard supply and some as low as 10 percent of the usual allowance within a couple of years of the disaster striking.[3]

Training was savaged and the bulk of the FAR was put to work on the economy, and agriculture and tourism in particular. Air force pilots were given tasks as pilots for tourist firms, army drivers for car hire companies, and naval personnel for yacht hire. More officers were sent to rapid courses in management techniques before being sent to head companies that desperately needed new approaches if they were to survive the times, or to others, often joint ventures with foreign investors, that would be needed desperately if the economy was to get out of its tailspin. Language qualifications almost certainly meant posting to fields other than traditional deterrence programs.

Fidel had early on said that the inevitably increased US pressure on the island in the wake of Soviet abandonment would necessitate that the FAR remain unaffected by the Special Period's exigencies.[4] But within a little over a year, Raul was obliged to cut the forces in half, their budget was left a shadow of itself (a drop from Cuban $1,149 million to $736.4 million, and even this figure was in Cuban pesos that were only a fraction of their former value), and their officer and NCO cadres picked clean of many good personnel.[5] The crisis was too deep for any other approach to be taken, whatever the level and immediacy of the external threat.

At the same time the FAR's proud links with the rest of the world, many of which were part of the results of Raúl's hard diplomatic work over decades, were shattered. Not only did Soviet intelligence cooperation nearly disintegrate, although the presence for a few more years of the Soviet and then Russian Lourdes Intelligence Complex meant that the collapse was not total or immediate, but also postings to the USSR and to Eastern Europe ended abruptly. Proper exercises also became a thing of the past, training courses in other countries and from officers of other countries ended, more sophisticated training nearly ended in many important spheres, and attaché positions with many embassies around the former Warsaw Pact and most of the Third World vanished. And even though Vietnam sent Havana its first advisers in that same year, the isolation was deeply felt. Cuba's armed forces went from being the most connected internationally of any in the Third World to having very little relations with the international community at all. And needless to say, a defense and deterrence posture based on the massive training of reservists suffered hugely from lack of training cadres, fuel, exercises, ammunition, and almost everything else required for its normal functioning. At the same time, the challenges professionally were tremendous, and in Exercise *Escudo Cubano* (Cuban Shield) that year, Fidel complained that Soviet influence had become too great and that in the face of US intransigence and determination to finally make an end of the Revolution, the FAR itself would have to do the work of survival and the original thinking to make that possible.[6]

The air force was especially hard hit, dependent as it is on highly trained personnel, especially pilots and repair technicians, and on sophisticated equipment and weapons. Some of the aircraft most needed for deterrence were kept at a high level of combat readiness but others could not be. Many pilots were no longer able to fly the normal hours required to maintain their skills. And many reserve pilots, vital for Cuba's deterrence strategy, were reduced from the usual one hundred to two hundred hours of flying time a year to a mere ten. While many pilots doing other jobs could be quickly brought back to normal military service, it was debatable in what condition they would be for doing their wartime or state-of-emergency job.[7]

The navy, which had been maintaining a limited "blue water" capacity in the escort and submarine fields, now essentially abandoned those roles. Instead, and significantly, it turned almost exclusively to employment that would be both more immediately useful to the Cuban state, and in this case, to the United States. The bulk of naval craft kept in active service were patrol boats with anti-illegal migration and antinarcotics roles. While these could be relatively quickly returned to deterrent tasks, their utility in these less traditional areas was great and earned dividends in pleasing important security sectors in the US government, not only the Pentagon but also the Drug Enforcement Agency (DEA) and the Coast Guard. This was a foreign policy support objective of enormous importance as it created within the US government elements that saw Cuba as a highly positive force and not one to be destroyed rapidly with no negative impact on the United States.

The air force also counted in this area, intercepting and tailing both aircraft and boats involved in the illegal drug trade and especially boats active in illegal migration. Odd as it might first seem, the army and especially the militia were also deeply engaged in major area sweeps, sometimes involving thousands of reservists, to find drug packages when a boat or aircraft was intercepted and "bombarded" Cuba or its surrounding waters or keys with them as it fled or made rendezvous with collaborators. The DEA, accustomed to far less cooperation from most Latin American and Caribbean "allies" of the United States could hardly be unimpressed, and its senior staff said so out loud.[8]

The army's role in such activities was significant but could not hide the fact that the land force was also damaged by the situation as a whole. While some units, vital for the deterrence role, were here again kept at a high level of readiness, a great many others were increasingly and almost exclusively used for agricultural roles essential to the nation's survival. Fidel first coined a phrase that Raúl then used constantly, "*Tanto valen los frijoles como los cañones*" (Beans are worth as much as cannons). By August 1994, Raúl could modify this phrase to "*Valen* más *los frijoles que los cañones*" (Beans are worth *more* than cannons).[9] In this he of course referred to the problems at home, which both brothers saw as first and foremost feeding the population.

Needless to say, the government was more than a little concerned about the internal security context with a population, accustomed to a reasonable standard of living, suddenly and for a very sustained period seeing that standard spiral downward. As mentioned, hunger and disease, not problems associated with Cuba for decades, again raised their heads on the island. There was every possibility that support for the regime, especially among the urban young, would collapse and see violence as a result. Given that the Tiananmen option was not a real one, and that the state was hardly going to give up its legitimacy, like the corrupt and apparatchik-ridden governments of Eastern Europe, without a fight, the only real option was to combat the problem by addressing the food and health problems directly.

Fidel had promised when the Special Period was declared that no hospital or school would close as a result of the crisis, however much it cost to keep them open. That promise held, and while the public health and education budgets dipped deeply in the first years of the crisis, they were to know nothing like the fall that the defense and security budget knew nor did they have to wait as long as that sector for a recovery of roughly previous levels of state investment. In this Fidel could count on the full support of Raúl, who made clear that he also felt that the only answer to the crisis was emphasis on food production and the acceptance of economic reforms that encouraged tourism, foreign investment, and a more open approach to trade.[10]

Slight Recovery but without the FAR as a Priority

The strategy worked, and despite disturbances in 1993 and 1994, including the very serious Habanazo riots of August of the latter year, neither the FAR nor even important police resources were ever needed in an internal security role. There was to be neither a Tiananmen Square nor a regime collapse in Cuba despite the prophecies of many Cuba-watchers, some even coming from journalists of the prestige of

Andrés Oppenheimer whose book on the island's future, written in 1991, had the extremely inappropriate title, *Castro's Final Hour*. This was erroneous or simply wishful thinking of the most ill-informed kind. By 1995, the economy was moving forward again, although slowly, and the worst of the Special Period, which was to last for several more years, was over.

The FAR was, however, expected to wait a good deal longer before it could expect any major improvement in its own situation. When other sectors, especially health and education, were already well on the mend, defense remained almost in free fall where budgets were concerned. But worse, the armed forces suffered further cuts in their strength as the Special Period carried on. By the middle of the decade, the forces were at a total strength of even less than one hundred thousand and by the end of the 1990s the International Institute for Strategic Studies presented a figure of only slightly over fifty-five thousand for all ranks, and this for a force standing at nearly five times that figure a decade previously.[11]

In addition, compulsory military service, while retained, was reduced from three years to two. This was a major change in a country that had counted on those three years of service to mold a real soldier who, even after years of retirement to the civilian world, would still be able to rapidly come back to his level of military efficiency of old, and would retain military values, as well. This was also the view of most traditional military thinking in Europe about the ideal period of time a conscript should spend in uniform before moving back to civilian life.

It is also possible to interpret these changes as sending a message to the United States that Cuba was not going to be engaged any longer in what Washington had seen as Havana's "adventurism" in the Third World and that even if it wished to, it would not be doing so in the future. Some see this in terms of hoping to assuage US ire and make the possibility of some sort of better relationship imaginable through showing that the export of revolution was now truly a thing of the past.[12] Be that as it may, the end in 1991 of any commitment in southern Africa was preceded the year before by the electoral defeat of the Sandinistas in Nicaragua and the end of Cuban cooperation with that country's armed forces. Cuba was thus disengaged as never before from internationalist military commitments, which it could ill afford in any case.

Two other points on this abandonment of the longer period of national service should be noted. First, the Cubans tried to make a virtue out of necessity on the issue. Since in any case the country could not afford the size of force that three years of full-blown conscription provided, the move was trumpeted as an achievement of the Revolution in the sense that the period of service could be reduced easily at this moment because Cuban youth were now better educated and included more technicians, qualified workers, and professionals, and thus not so many of them were needed in the FAR at any one time. The FAR also emphasized that troops were now back from abroad, and that women serving in the *Servicio Militar Voluntario Femenino* (Women's Voluntary Military Service), one of Raúl and Vilma's most beloved schemes, were reducing the need for such a long period of service for male youth.[13]

The second point to keep in mind here is that with the regular force reduced to hardly more than fifty thousand men, it simply was unnecessary to have young men serve for as long as they had had to do when the force to be manned was five times that size. In addition, many more young males were staying in the FAR when their time of service ended as a result of its comparative advantages when looked at in the context of the labor market in Cuba at the time, and the many perks of service.

Equipment and weapons stocks remained relatively steady, but the requirement to keep vital systems working and to undertake the myriad roles assigned in the Special Period meant that a process of deep "cannibalization,"—that is, the taking of spare parts from some weapons or vehicles to allow others to function—was inevitably put in place. Spare parts acquisition thus became, along with repairs, a vital need and the new Russian policy of "cash and carry," rather than simply generous donation, where Cuba was concerned, meant that essentially nothing at all was bought on the open arms market. The sight of Raúl reviewing a parade of quite sophisticated antiaircraft guns being towed literally by bicycles, while clearly demonstrating Cuba's determination to continue defending itself, also showed the desperate straits to which it had been driven. Here again the navy and air force were even more stricken than the army.

This analyst could not help noticing one thing about the situation that, while not unique historically, was nearly so. Normally when what must be considered in a Western sense as an authoritarian regime faces a deep and enduring crisis at the political, social, and economic level, it reacts by strengthening its defense and security forces. However, such was the confidence of the government that the state would hold firm despite the horrors of the moment, that in the Cuban case, the FAR was arguably the most called-upon element of the state to make sacrifices seeing its strength and capacities more

diminished during the crisis than any other part of the state structure. It is noteworthy that this occurred, despite the visible growth
of the threat to that state at the time. For example, the percentage
of the state budget given over to defense and security in 1990 was
7.1 percent, before the disaster struck. Its lowest percentage reached
over these years, a mere 3.9 percent, was immediately after the disturbances of 1993/4 when the threat seemed greatest.[14] Fidel could
be proud of this stability and endurance, and Raúl could be equally
so for his part in delivering to the state an apparatus as loyal and flexible as the armed forces.

It had not been easy. If the overall strength of the armed forces had
fallen by a huge factor, the blow to the officer corps was even more
impressive. Given the nature of the reserve and mobilization system
of the Guerra de Todo el Pueblo, the officer corps had always been
kept high in numbers and quality. While it is true that most reserve
units would in action have reserve commanders, as elsewhere in the
world, a large mobilization base must to some extent depend also
on extra regular officers ready to take their place in charge of larger
formations, beefed up by reservists, and more extensive operations in
time of emergency.

A large officer corps, however, in the circumstances of the Special
Period, could simply not be afforded. Thousands of officers were
not to be needed, and these were of course in most cases career
officers in a professional armed force who logically were planning
to make those careers in their chosen field and organization. Here
again Raúl showed great ingenuity in dealing with problems of bottlenecks in promotion and other issues that could easily have power-
fully threatened the institution and its cohesion at a time when it was
vital to show officers that they would be taken care of in the difficult
moments at hand.

The growing role of the FAR in the economy as a whole was a
huge help in this regard. As we have seen, the FAR has always had
an unusual place in the national economy, exceeding the standards of
other countries and armed forces in Latin America. From victory in
1959 and even before in the war in Oriente, the FAR had been ordered
to take on agricultural and industrial production jobs. And this had
never been abandoned entirely, even during the Sovietization and
enhanced professionalization period of the late 1960s and 1970s.

This longstanding tradition had been reinforced if changed with
the need for officers in larger numbers trained in modern management techniques as of the *perfeccionamiento* (improvement) campaign
of the mid 1980s. That experience, both recent and further back, was

now to stand the FAR in very good stead indeed as its role in the economy, and especially in its most dynamic sectors, took off in the early 1990s. The first parts of this move did not appear to be limited to dynamic sectors. A "soldier's soldier" and known for being especially close to Raúl, Major-General Ulises Rosales del Toro was chosen in 1997 to head the *Ministerio del Azúcar* (Ministry of Sugar), a key ministry in the government and in a sector that had long been ailing but was now in desperate shape with low yields and low prices for what was produced by the vast cane fields of the island. Rosales del Toro was particularly well-viewed by Raúl for his role in the thinking behind the Guerra de Todo el Pueblo strategy but was also well-known for his constant calls from the beginning of the Special Period for increasing not decreasing the professional standards of the officer corps.

The general had recently been sent by Raúl to Europe, the highest ranking Cuban officer to be so employed, to take business management courses.[15] There could have been no more powerful signal that the government was intending to tackle its economic woes with seriousness and would make extensive use of the FAR to do so.

He was only one, however, of those sent to other sectors to bring them into more productivity through the application of a mix of military and modern business approaches. The Cubanacán tourism services chain, the Habaneros tobacco enterprise, and the then Cuban-Italian joint venture telephone company ETECSA all received senior officers at the director level. The Fisheries and Merchant Marine Ministry and others, with less obvious connections to defense, were also for some time headed by senior officers temporarily seconded to them. It is difficult to exaggerate the central importance of these postings to key industries as part of the survival strategy of the state in the Special Period and Raúl's role in advising Fidel as to the right man for the job, so often seen before in this story, was rarely more needed than over this period.

The FAR set up in connection with all this—and rather quickly pushing aside in importance the more military, production-oriented *Unión de Industrias Militares* (UIM)—a more profitable and much more dollar-linked *Grupo de Administracion Empresarial, SA* (Business Administration Group or GAESA-) and placed it under General Julio Casas Regueiro, the first vice-minister of MINFAR and a close colleague of Raúl.[16] This should not be seen as meaning that the UIM was shunted aside entirely. It remained essential for production and repair for FAR military needs.[17] But the UIM did not bring in significant foreign currency to the state, so it could not expect to see its influence grow like that of GAESA, whose executive officer became no less central, or trusted, a figure than Raúl's own son-in-law Luis Alberto Rodríguez, also a serving FAR officer. Raúl was not only putting in place people in whom he had confidence as professional managers but ones in whom he had personal confidence for their loyalty. Just as in 1959 when loyal Ejército Rebelde officers had been chosen for key administrative jobs in the face of the challenges of running the country without a loyal bureaucracy and manager class, so in the 1990s FAR officers were charged in the context of a new crisis of administration to do the same. The difference was a direct result of Raúl's administration of the FAR over those years; this time they would not only be loyal but competent in their functions, as well.

For the purposes of this part of our study, however, it was the importance of these business activities in allowing the FAR to place "excess" but promising officers in positions of importance and responsibility that is perhaps most telling. Hundreds of officers, instead of simply facing retirement in these very difficult times, were given new and testing jobs and a large number could be retained in uniform while taking on such employment. Indeed, giving them these positions while they were still serving in the forces was considered essential as they could then remain active and subject to military discipline and justice until their retirement, thus remaining visibly military; additionally, the government could avoid the accusation of giving plum civilian jobs to former military officers.[18]

Other officers and senior NCOs retired to the national police force (Policia Nacional Revolucionaria or PNR). While at first not expanded, the national police soon faced a crime wave set off by growing tourism and the crisis in general. In January 1999, Fidel announced both a major expansion of the police and improvements in their conditions of service and pay. And some other officers found their way into MININT, still feeling the impact of the Ochoa Affair and the subsequent purge brought on by it.

Even with all these efforts, however, many officers still faced compulsory retirement in an economic context of great strain. Just as important perhaps, almost all officers who remained in active service found themselves facing serious bottlenecks for promotion. One could simply not cut a military force by these percentages and expect promotions and advancement in general to remain attractive. Here it can only be surmised that it was the morale, sense of duty, professionalism, and urgency of the situation that allowed the FAR to carry on with such drive in all their assigned tasks.

And carry on they did. In all the natural disasters that have struck Cuba in these years, the FAR has been present and indeed the decisive organizational element in fighting their effects and keeping Cuba as the model for most of the world where natural disaster preparation and relief are concerned. Raúl's own role in the setting up of the *Sistema de Defensa Civil de Cuba* (Civil Defense System of Cuba), dependent first in part and then directly on MINFAR, now paid off as despite cuts the system continued to work in years of strikingly increased threats from the effects of disasters, especially those caused by Cuba's national plague of hurricanes. While personnel available for such roles have obviously been less numerous than in the halcyon days of the FAR, they have continued their central role of coordination of the national effort in this area of activity.[19]

The deterrent system, deeply wounded by scarcities in everything needed for mass training, has nonetheless remained in place. Key units have been kept up to the requirements for wartime. And if equipment, weapon, manpower, and training standards have not been kept to the same levels as in the past, the reserve forces remain impressive and ubiquitous as well as frequently employed for everything from drug seizures to natural disaster situations. Their weaknesses would probably only come out in any attempts to use them massively and in coordinated traditional roles. However, even here it is just these problems that recent defense efforts such as Bastión 2009 and *Operación Cabaiguán* (Operation Cabaiguan) are meant at least in part to address.[20]

In this, Raúl has been active throughout. Until his elevation to the acting presidency on July 31, 2006, and his election in February 2008, he was constantly visiting units, clamoring for reports, speaking to officers, NCOs, and soldiers alike, asking often very direct questions and expecting frank answers. And while this was always his style as commander and minister, it has been all the more visible as the difficult recent times took their toll on efficiency and well-being. Officers and other ranks alike refer all the time to his presence over these years in their units and training centers and his willingness to listen to their problems and attempt to address them.[21]

Comments about his service as minister during the Special Period, from senior officers who know Raúl well, are legion and virtually all concur. And if it is true that these officers are not likely to criticize their superior directly, there is a common thread here that is worth noting as it coincides with what one hears from virtually all who have served in the FAR over these years, whether their comments were public or private and in confidence.

General Néstor López Cuba, for example, in an interview, puts emphasis on Raúl's immediate call for officers to answer to certain needs that are quite original for Latin America and expresses well the challenges of the Special Period. He says:

> Raúl put forward to the senior ranks of the armed forces four requirements. First, they had to be political cadres with high political, ideological and moral qualities. Second, that they had to be highly prepared military professionals. Third, that they master the rudiments of food production and agriculture. And fourth that they master rudimentary economics.[22]

He expects them to comply fully. General Harry Villegas refers to these same exigencies. "Raúl is very strict, very fair, but he demands of his subordinates that they answer for their errors."[23] Raúl soon insisted as well on officers agreeing to abide by a new code of ethics in the context of the temptations many were facing for the first time and in the terrible conditions of the Special Period. It seems that he holds them very much to account for their continued compliance with this code, as well.[24]

Perhaps, however, it is General José Ramón Fernández who sums up best the general view of the man in this period and throughout his career; he says:

> Raúl is a man like other men. Energetic, but extraordinarily affable, he has a very Cuban character, with a great ability to communicate with the people, he loves his children, is able to tell stories, to make jokes and to join in on them. (He is able) to talk to this person, to go to the home of another, ... he is very sincere saying things and is a person of profound sensitivity when dealing with other men. He has lots of friends, and knows how to be a friend, how to be a father, how to be a companion, and he knows how to be a firm and demanding political and military leader.[25]

If there is one word that constantly comes up in describing Raúl, it is this last one, *exigente* (demanding), with others but also with himself. In facing the Special Period, any other approach would have found little relevance if the FAR were to operate properly and as an example to others.

The Vexing Issue of Corruption

No subject is as troubling to the leadership of the Cuban government as that of corruption. The legitimacy of that government and leadership is in no small measure a direct result of its campaign in the early years after 1959 against the kind of corruption that Cuba had always known but which had become perhaps even more endemic with the Batista dictatorship. The reputation of the FAR was especially high in this regard, and it was largely Ejército Rebelde officers who spearheaded the successful clean-up of 1959 through 1961. Cuba cannot say that it never, as a revolutionary state, had any corruption at senior levels, but it can claim to have eradicated that which it found, not fallen into the patterns of corruption found in Eastern Europe's socialist states, and vitally, not allow any hint of impunity on the issue.

Such was the depth and breadth of the crisis termed the Special Period, however, that lower levels of corruption were to come back to Cuba as a generalized phenomenon, in order just to get by, which often shook and continues to shake people's confidence in the state, the government, the political leadership, and the socialist system as a whole. And given the massive role of the armed forces in the economy, and especially in its most dynamic sectors, it was inevitable that at least to some extent even as popular and respected an institution as the FAR would come in for some public criticism.

This survival mentality and related corruption in Cuba is generalized but perhaps not as easily understood as elsewhere in Latin America. For a start, it is probably not as visible at the top of the system as it is at the bottom, not a phenomenon common elsewhere. Secondly, as in much of the world, it is often not seen as corruption in the full sense but as a way of making things work in a stressed system where they often do not, and also in Cuba as a way of surviving decently in a system where the official wage does not allow such a condition to prevail. In Cuba, the common verb used for making something happen that otherwise would not is *resolver* (to resolve). One asks for someone else who can "resolver" something for me, and it is understood that this will be done in unorthodox, usually vaguely or even directly illegal ways.

The major scarcities that characterized Cuban life in the worst years of the Special Period (and to some extent still do) were so widespread as to make it necessary for everyone to try to get things through a system of mutual help. Much of this could be done via family and friendship connections but much of it could not. Thus networks of resolution of problems built up within the wider social framework and permitted people to resolve things outside the shattered rationing system, agricultural supply system, clothing acquisition arrangements, and so on. The system worked largely without cash exchanged but not entirely so. For someone resolving something for another person, it was possible but not usual, under the prevailing ethic, for one to compensate him or her with *un regalito* (a little gift), or *un recuerdo* (a souvenir)—that is, a small bribe.

To some it would seem almost silly to raise such an issue. After all, in most cases it would take the form of a policeman turning a blind eye to an old lady asking illegally for a coin from a tourist or a similar person shining shoes without a license. In return, the policeman would not get a cash bribe and certainly would not get very much in return, but he might expect every week to be handed a regalito in the form of a soft drink or a small item from the person being overlooked. This worked for everything touching government administration as well, especially if it involved the tourist or other "dollar" parts of the economy as it must be remembered that the Cuban economy is dual in the sense that normal salaries are paid in pesos *moneda nacional* ("national money, " which cannot be converted into foreign currency, as opposed to the peso *convertible*, which can), which are worth roughly four US cents at the moment—however, a great many items can only be purchased with pesos convertibles. These convertible pesos are not part of the usual pay packet that most Cubans have access to but must be obtained by *remesas* (remittances) from abroad, dealings (often illegal) with tourists or other foreigners, or the black market.

In another system, none of this would necessarily touch the armed forces, but in Cuba, where the FAR has such a gigantic role in the economy and the nation as a whole, it can and does. A sergeant working in a military-run cement factory will have access to bags of cement which have, in the jargon of resolver, "fallen off the back of a truck." He can then, if he can get them out safely and secretly from the factory, sell them or exchange them for other goods or services in the resolver system to someone else who has access to things he in turn needs or wants. Thus at the bottom of the military system, given its place in society, there is more room for "corruption" than one might normally expect.

Since, however, most everyone is involved in the resolver system, there is little negative reaction to the sergeant doing his illegal dealings in cement as long as it is not excessive. After all, so the reasoning goes, he cannot live decently on what he makes and thus is obliged to get involved just like virtually everyone else. What is more commented upon is when it is assumed or known that this is happening rather higher up the chain of command.

One must be quite clear on this. There is virtually no one who imagines that Fidel or Raúl is involved in any such things. US suggestions that Fidel or anyone else in the *cúpula* somehow has stashes of money in accounts abroad, along the Latin American dictatorial model, are laughed at almost across the board in Cuba. The men at the top have shown through their own blood and courage that they are not about to abandon the Revolution and run off to a more comfortable retired life in a friendly country in Africa, Asia, or Latin America if and when things get tough. Rightly or wrongly, they are much more likely to die in the saddle, and such is the likelihood of this being the case here that it has become the general view in Cuba on this matter. Even those who dislike the regime intensely have difficulty believing that it will be abandoned by its leaders if times get harder or more dangerous. After all, those times have come before and no one in the high leadership of the nation has left what seemed a sinking ship. Certainly nothing that we know of Raúl would suggest that he is going anywhere but the trenches if things were to go very badly.

What some Cubans do believe is that in the generalized context of prevailing corruption, a general who has control of a state enterprise, even more so a mixed enterprise with a foreign company, a ministry, or the like somehow *must* be taking advantage of his position to enrich himself or more likely to at least make his life a little more comfortable. It should also be clear that Cubans do not in any way think the armed forces are more inclined to do this than other sectors. This is not Central America or the Andes, and entirely the opposite is true. Cubans usually think their armed forces are less inclined to take part than anyone else in corrupt practices but that nonetheless they may well do so because there is no other real option for them any more than there is for any other Cuban who wishes to live decently.

They also sometimes feel that less senior officers, but ones with a good *pincho* (job that has advantages) because of their training in business management or just because they are in a position of that kind, must also be taking advantage in some fashion. They do not necessarily begrudge them this advantage but do often feel most definitely that it is exercised in the same illegal but necessary fashion that they use.

Raúl, Fidel, and the FAR command rail against the charge but also against the practice, meaning that whether they like it or not, they realize that it is a problem. Raúl has within the FAR, MININT, CDRs, and the multiple security and other organizations that responded to him as minister of the armed forces, organized literally thousands of courses on corruption, how to fight it, how to search it out and report it, and the like.[26]

Perhaps more importantly, his reaction to high-level corruption has since the beginning of the Special Period been swift and fierce. Senior officers, including at least one general, have not only been sacked but dismissed with disgrace from the forces, lost all rights to a pension, stripped of their rank and decorations, and of course jailed for long terms for having engaged in corruption. Raúl has also set up elements of the armed forces security and intelligence system that are specifically tasked with addressing this challenge and work hard to trace any such developments in the officer corps, especially those close to the dollar economy. But the opportunities are many and difficult to resist even if the dangers and probable sanctions are real and serious. Senior officers are certainly not immune to temptation as is so often the case in Latin America, but they know that Cuba has an extra weapon in finding the guilty out.[27]

This weapon is the Cuban himself or herself. Cuban senior officers in many interviews and conversations have said that even if they wanted to engage in such activities, the "national sport,"—that is, gossiping and watching what other people are doing, both heightened pastimes in the years of the Special Period—would keep them from doing so.[28] They claim with vigor that while anyone else can get a new refrigerator without undue comment from the neighbors, they would be watched like hawks and become the common discussion point for the whole neighborhood in which they live if they were to do so. There is of course something to this. In a very socially active society like Cuba's, it would be difficult indeed to hide ill-gotten ostentatious signs of wealth from public view. But the complaint is often not that the gains are ostentatious but rather that they are carefully hidden from view for later enjoyment.

A word must be said about the social and other origins of the officer corps at this time. If Raúl is very much the "other" in comparison to other commanding generals and military presidents in Latin America, the FAR's officer corps is at least equally different. By law, one half of the intake annually of cadets to the Camilo Cienfuegos armed forces cadet schools that prepare young people for military academy later on must be sons and daughters of workers or peasants, a situation simply unthinkable anywhere else in Latin America or perhaps the world. This ensures that the usual Latin American officer corps made up overwhelmingly of the children of former or still serving officers and NCOs is avoided actively by policy in Cuba. It also means that blacks and mulatos are well represented in the officer corps, if not necessarily at the highest rank levels.

It must also be remembered that the historic leadership of the FAR is equally rooted in working-class or lower-middle-class families and origins. There are no signs of sons or daughters of the wealthy at all in the FAR's senior ranks. And if this has meant that there is also less formal learning among them, it is not because the forces have not tried since 1959 to change the situation. But an understanding that it is still the case is very widespread in the FAR leadership and something they often say they are trying to change.[29]

When the insurrection was raging against Batista in the late 1950s the clash, while far from a mere Marxist class struggle at its most simple, was often between the have and have-not Cubans. Fidel and Raúl were in that sense the exceptions, coming from quite a wealthy family. The vast majority of those who chose self-exile in the first years of the new government did so because their upper-class status meant that they stood to lose the most from the Revolution and indeed often did. And in the context of the racial situation in the United States of the time as well as the place of blacks and mulatos in the society and economy of Cuba, members of those racial groups were most unlikely to leave.

This led in the Special Period, some 40 years later, to the present situation wherein the bulk of those receiving remesas from abroad tend to be from those very groups that are least favorable to the Revolution. There are enormous numbers of exceptions to this situation, and if United Nations figures are to be believed, the majority of Cubans, given the level of emigration over the last decades, now have access to some hard currency coming in one form or another from abroad. But be that as it may groups that have tended to be especially loyal to the Revolution tend also to be those that have least access to these vital sources of convertible pesos.

It is they who have had members of their families emigrate less often. And it is they who have worked hardest for the Revolution, tended more often to join its militias and other security forces, and even mistreated on occasion those who wished to leave the island or at least not support its revolutionary experiment. Little wonder that they are shocked and disappointed when it turns out generally to be the families that are least active in being *revolucionarios* who are doing best in the present situation. And this situation has been exacerbated by the current reform process which has stimulated such a vast increase in new small businesses and larger farming plots. For the exploitation of such improvements requires capital and generally if one has no access to remesas, one's chances of exploiting the new rules are not good.

The armed forces, police, MININT, and other security forces of course tend to recruit from just these most loyalist sectors of the population. And it is those sectors that have suffered most, not least, from the Special Period. The potential of this situation to lead to security forces personnel engaging in some activities of an illegal kind in order to get closer to an even keel with those they see as their less loyal compatriots is, not surprisingly, very high.

It is important not to exaggerate here. One hears of nothing like the level and breadth of corruption in the Policía Nacional Revolucionaria that is reported in Argentina, most of Central America, the Dominican Republic, Mexico, Paraguay, the central Andean countries, or Venezuela. Cubans are in no sense suffering from state security forces corruption in the way most Latin Americans do. But as so often in Cuba there is a tendency for the country to be the victim of its own successes. The fact that corruption was virtually wiped out in the first years of the revolutionary experiment means that Cubans became accustomed to a state that functioned with a lack of the scourge that was so widespread and infamous in most of the region.

It cannot be said that this reputation remains although in many ways it should. It is a risky business indeed to attempt to suborn a policeman in Cuba even today, not at all the situation in many countries of the region. Actual systematic extortion from protection rackets or the like is unknown as opposed to the practice one sees in much of Latin America. "Regalitos" tend to be absurdly small and related to the bureaucrat's own requirement to resolver and not to a massive system of exploitation by the powerful of the weak. In many ways, what impresses one in the highly difficult context in which Cubans live today is how little real corruption there is, and not how much.

It is Raúl's armed forces, however, that are the subject here, and it is undeniable that many serving personnel at lower levels have fallen into the more negative elements of the resolver system and have used their positions to profit improperly. Control of the important *Tiendas de Recaudación de Divisas* (Foreign Exchange Collection Stores or TRD), where imported goods, especially some electrical appliances, are available for purchase in pesos convertibles, has led to cases of abuse of position. Ministerial and corporate positions have also presented their temptations to which a minority of officers have not been able to resist. And all ranks with access to material goods of value have been tempted by the option of stealing and selling or exchanging them for goods or favors they need. Once again, perhaps one should be surprised by how little and not by how often personnel yield to such temptations.

Raúl and the armed forces leadership do not, however, see it in that light. One option to deal with the matter has been to improve the lot of the serviceman and police personnel. And it must be said that there are real perks to military or police service. There are frequent opportunities in which security forces personnel have legal and normal access to the goods sold at the TRD. The difference is that they have such access in pesos moneda nacional terms. Instead of paying for them in pesos convertibles (worth officially one dollar each and difficult to obtain for many Cubans), they can buy on occasion the same goods for the same number of pesos moneda nacional.

In addition, most but not all armed forces installations have officers' and senior NCOs' messes and other rank canteens, similar to those in many other countries, where drinks and food can be purchased at greatly reduced prices. Also as in most other countries, those bases offer swimming pools, admittedly rarely luxurious ones, and other leisure activities to service personnel and their families. And while it is true that most Cuban towns have such amenities available for all inhabitants, they are rarely in as good repair or as little crowded as the FAR or MININT ones. Military hospitals also tend to be better supplied and run than civilian ones, although this advantage may be slackening since most patients there during the Special Period (and with the reduction of the strength of the armed forces) have been civilians and not serving military personnel.[30]

Salaries have also improved greatly for the security forces especially for the police. And if those salaries are paid only in moneda nacional, they do go further than they would for persons who do not have the additional perks mentioned. Thus one method for combating corruption has been with what in most countries would be considered perfectly normal defense and security forces advantages.

As seen, another powerful means is making it so that no one enjoys impunity from prosecution if they are found guilty of ill-doing in this sense. And yet another is to make sure the punishments meted out are great disincentives to going the route of corruption. All of these play their role. Perks can be seen as the last of these. As can be imagined, however, this situation does not put senior officers or other pinchos out of the reach of adverse public comment even if it does normally do so with more junior officers of lieutenant-colonel and below rank, who very rarely indeed are criticized by the public for doing excessively well or living off the system.

Senior officers are quick to defend themselves and argue forcefully that they do not live better than other Cubans and that if they tried to do so, *el chisme cubano* (the infamous Cuban tradition of constant gossiping) would make it impossible for them to do so in any case. One is sometimes in a position of thinking they "do protest too much" on this score. Some defenses are surely exaggerated but most contain a great deal of truth. General Néstor López Cuba has said that in the FAR, "We have never permitted corruption. In that we are intransigent. The military must stay free from any personal interest."[31] From there came Raúl's own new orders in 1990 requiring the officer corps to be even more attentive to these problems because of the Special Period's challenges, and there are now instructions, as we have seen, that retiring officers may not have access to positions in *empresas mixtas* (the new mixed enterprises spawned by the Special Period's opening up to the world economy). Referring to the new code imposed by Raúl, General Enrique Carreras has said, "These norms are essential if the public is to support the personnel and leaders of the Revolution. Because this is a small people- we are 11 million—but very observant. People look to see how you live. Thus we don't have to point out abuses to anyone because the people themselves will, and will begin to fight those leaders." And General Villegas has added with some truth, even if with considerable exaggeration as well, "Every time there is a need for a control cadre of propriety one looks for a member of the FAR. They are educated to be an example of austerity, honesty and honor." Even Fidel, Villegas shows, has come to the defense of the military on this issue saying, "It is a source of pride not to have a single member of the armed forces who is rich. No one who retires has privileges that others in Cuba do not have . . . you won't find one that has got rich in the armed forces."[32]

These are of course comments that one would expect from the senior officers themselves, although some of their colleagues do admit to there being a problem here.[33] But it is also clear that the FAR do work hard to deal with corruption, that officers do tend to be honest, that education in the military stresses continually this point, and that it is difficult in the extreme in Cuba to avoid public detection and highly negative comment if one lives high on the hog. Perhaps more telling still is that in conversations with any number of senior foreign executives working with Cuban senior and not so senior officers in or on empresas mixtas issues, the overwhelming opinion is that those officers are generally honest and that the dubious approaches foreign firms have to take in most of the rest of Latin America rarely apply in Cuba.

In any case, as in all corruption the fact is that it is the level of punishment and impunity that are most important in combating the problem.[34] And when General Tomás Benítez, head of the Gaviota tourism chain, was found guilty of corruption and accepting bribes, he was fired and imprisoned with a long sentence. When likewise two full colonels from the *Ministerio de Comercio Interior* (Ministry of Internal Commerce) were discovered to be involved in fraud, they were likewise dismissed and sent to jail. There is doubtless some corruption in the higher ranks of the armed forces, but no one can say that there is impunity or that there is no attempt to deal with the problem. And the current heightened anticorruption campaign has struck hard at senior officers who have forgotten this state of affairs.

Raúl is the man who has been most active in addressing the issue not only by setting up codes of conduct or organizing courses on the problem, but by speaking frequently to officers on the need to be vigilant. Because it is clear that General Carreras's comments above are indeed accurate, and that the legitimacy of the regime must come in good part from its extraordinary record in reducing corruption. If the situation worsens and takes an even greater toll on the public, and if the FAR are seen to be part of the problem and not the solution, the weakening of public confidence in the central pillar of the state could eventually be serious indeed. Fortunately for Cuba, we still seem to be far from that situation, but it is still the case that this problem must be watched with care.

Chapter 5

Partial Recovery and
Last Years as Minister

By 1995, most economists observing Cuba agreed, the nation had "bottomed out" and the slightest of recoveries had begun. The measures taken to encourage large-scale tourism, foreign investment, diversification of trade, and allowance of limited *cuenta propismo* (small-scale private enterprises) for hundreds of thousands of Cubans seemed to have done their work. For several years, Cuba would know impressive growth rates, although judged against a very shrunken economy previously, and there would be a visible improvement in everything from stocks of goods in shops to generally in families' acquisitive capacity; additionally, there would be a reduction in the costly and intensely frustrating effects of widespread *apagones* (electricity blackouts) in the conditions of the Special Period.[1]

As mentioned, the FAR did not see these positive effects as quickly as some other ministries and especially those of public health and education despite Raúl's efforts to soften the blows to his own institution. Its budget continued to decline and its numerical strength did not even begin to recover its previous position. Even when in 1997 there was a slight increase in the budget, that increase was a measure to stave off disaster and was not to prove anything like a trend. For in 1998, the budget fell back sharply again. Indeed, ten years after the beginning of the Special Period, in 2000, with the general economic recovery well under way for half a decade, the defense and security budget was still at only 75 percent of its 1990 level. Only with 2001 did the trend toward a truly recovering budget in this sector begin, and even then it is important to remember we are still looking at moneda nacional figures of a vastly devalued peso generally of only about 4 percent of its previous value.[2]

Priority was clearly still going to other ministries and Raúl was active in designing the policies that made this so, given his certainty that the only answer to the dangers to the Revolution inherent in the crisis was economic recovery and most decidedly not any type of recourse to military force. The FAR as a whole was still expected to contribute to the harvest—the EJT to give itself over entirely to that role—to deploy resources to run key elements of the economy, to support foreign policy goals, to run natural disaster preparation and relief, and to continue to deter attack. It would have been a heavy burden for any military system, but in the straits in which the FAR found itself it was tremendous. In addition the Tropas de Milicias Territoriales were expected to be self-financing through their other, nonmilitary roles and the FAR as a whole to cost the national treasury the absolute minimum.

The height of the crisis of the Special Period may have been past but its very length and continued severity meant that the danger of a social explosion could not be ignored entirely. MININT's Special Forces offered a partial guarantee but obviously such a small force could not ensure entirely the regime's security if things got out of hand. Despite this situation, the FAR did not even begin riot control or other minor internal security training as a great many armies, including those of western democracies, did and do on a virtually routine basis.

Training, weaponry, and equipment matters were not so easily resolved. Cannibalization of some weapons and equipment to provide key units with the essentials for a deterrence and operational posture continued at an even heavier pace as the years wore on. Training remained better than might be expected but was still poor when compared with the standards of recent decades. Many personnel in the conscripted ranks complained of boredom and sloth because of the lack of stimulating training and the huge requirement for simple laborers for the harvest.

At the same time some disturbing trends emerged. The combination of less need to take in such a large percentage of male youth, a shorter period of service, and the general stresses of the moment produced a much wider and worrying diversity in the range of military capability and experience in the male population than had been the case for some time. Some young men were doing regular conscripted service with front-line units and had very good training of the traditional type for that unit's roles. Others were spending the full time with the army but not with front-line units and with less than good training. Still others were doing only the five-week *previa* basic training course and then were sent to either the EJT or some other job where they had little further military training at all. And there were even some who appear to have escaped even the previa and could not be said to have had any real training to speak of.

When this is added to the large group of young men who chose, or were chosen for MININT, firemen, customs officials, social services, and the myriad other options of "national service" or combined education/service arrangements, it is clear that the oft-heard boast of a "nation in arms" was being watered down more than somewhat. Many members of the youth of these years escaped service altogether, or did so little, or what they did was so unlike normal military service that the reserve force, for the first time, began to look less serious. The FAR, and Raúl in particular, was aware of the danger, but it was not possible to address the whole range of problems that arose given the current numerical strength, the reduced budget for defense, and the massive demands being made on the institution.

The FAR and the International Context

If internal trends were not that favorable, the FAR had little time to become fixated on them. The relationship with the United States went from bad to worse following the passage of the 1992 Torricelli Act after looking for a while as if it might actually improve. President Bill Clinton, while having mixed views on Cuba, was a Democrat and had opposed some of the harsher stands against the island of the previous decades. His arrival in power in 1993 therefore made optimists feel that some progress might be made under his administration.

They were wrong. Conditions on the island were such that thousands of Cubans were emigrating to the north illegally and several disasters at sea occurred with considerable loss of life in 1994. Washington was using, at least as far as the Cuban government was concerned, US noncompliance with bilateral migration accords to pressure Havana even further at this difficult time. Castro's reaction in August 1994, less than a week after the Habanazo rioting, was to announce that he would allow anyone who wished to leave the island to do so without hindrance. Thousands more *balseros* did just that. In a humiliating retreat, the US government agreed to a new migration accord one month later. The accords not only recognized the Cuban government's legitimacy but provided for reasonably high-level meetings between Havana and Washington on a regular basis at least every six months. Fidel was delighted and Raúl, who, all observers agree, had been arguing throughout the crisis that reactions to popular displeasure involving the armed forces were simply not think-able options, could breathe a sigh of relief.

The situation worsened dramatically, however, in February 1996. For some time there had been a bill pending in Congress to codify the edicts, regulations, laws, decrees, and the like that made up the US embargo against Cuba. This legislation, proposed by extremist members of Congress and termed the Helms-Burton Bill, was being held up by opposition to it in the Congress, and it was fairly certain that it might be vetoed, even if it were passed, by the new president. It did not look like it had much chance of passing in any case because it not only called for codifying all former rules that made up the "blockade," thus making them law and not changeable by executive action, but likewise abolished the president's prerogative in foreign policy by making it illegal for a US government to negotiate with a Cuban government in which Fidel or Raúl were ministers. In addition to these truly exceptional provisions, it provided for punishing for-eign firms that "trafficked" in nationalized properties and proposed other measures that were visibly, in legal terms, "extra-territorial" in both tone and effect.[3]

Meanwhile, another issue was vexing the Cubans and particularly the armed forces. For years, boats and aircraft had been leaving US ports and airports in the south with a view to going to Cuba and engaging in counterrevolutionary activities. Some of these undertook terrorist tasks such as sabotage and firing bazookas and other arms at hotels where foreign tourists were staying, this in order to deter such visits to Cuba and starve the Cuban state of the funds com-ing from them. Others dropped leaflets on Cuban towns denounc-ing the government and calling for Cubans to rise up against the government. The US administration, doubtless to avoid an unpleas-ant backlash from Cuban-Americans, simply did nothing about it, although Washington acknowledged that it was of course against international law.

To say the least, the FAR was less than impressed, and Raúl spoke on several occasions to the subject. Knowing they had the capability to stop at least the aircraft and perhaps the boats as well, they wanted to show the groups doing this that they could not invade Cuban sov-ereign air and sea space with impunity. For some time, MINREX had been advising Washington that this activity would not be toler-ated and that the US government would need to act to put a stop to it. Nothing was ever done. And when a particularly daring group, Brothers to the Rescue, persisted in penetrating Cuban air space, and the warning to the United States to do something about them was yet again ignored, the *Fueza Aérea Revolucionaria*, Cuba's air force, was ordered to shoot two offending aircraft down and this its Migs did, killing in the act the aircrafts' pilots.

The storm that this set off in the United States was exceptional and the immediate result was the passage of the Helms-Burton Bill. The trend toward majority opinion in the United States favoring normalization of relations, developing for some years in that country, ended in a flood of condemnation of the FAR's actions and even of Raúl personally with his reputation in the United States for ruthlessness reinforced. The institution might have been increasingly engaged in economic and other activities, but it had not forgotten its defense of sovereignty role or the fact that it was the guarantor of national independence. The decision was clearly made at the highest level. But the political cost was high and the economic one, with the bill's passage, was to be high, as well.

Over the same years, the evolution of defense thinking in the United States on the nature of the Cuban threat was taking an interesting turn. Pentagon analysts had never taken a specifically Cuban threat very seriously in war planning. Instead, the Cuban Navy and Air Force were seen as potentially annoying factors in the logistics problems the United States would have to face in case of a major war with the Soviet Union in Europe. Cuba of course sits astride the Florida Straits and various Bahamian channels that US shipping might be using in order to reinforce the European theater of war in such a situation, and if Cuba were supporting the USSR in such a conflict, not a certain state of affairs of course, its forces could damage shipping coming from the Gulf of Mexico ports or even to some degree through the Panama Canal. While Pentagon thinking did not consider that Cuba could make much trouble in this way, it could add one more negative factor to the US calculations and war effort.

With the winding down of the Cold War, US strategic thought began to take Cuba even less seriously. It was after all clear that Moscow and Havana did not have a collective security accord in any traditional sense and that the Soviets at least were unlikely in the extreme to help Cuba if the island were attacked. Thus some Pentagon reasoning suggested that Cuba would not by any means feel itself obliged to come to the aid of the Soviets in case of their becoming embroiled in conflict with the United States, especially when that would mean the end of the Cuban Revolution, the Castro government, and perhaps of national independence itself. It did not seem that in any sense such a game could be worth the candle for Cuba.

In any case, the Cold War was ending and such calculations were less telling in light of a shift of attention in the United States from traditional defense concerns such as the Soviet threat to nontraditional challenges and especially their recently assigned role in fighting the illegal narcotics trade, a role where Cuban assistance might be interesting for the United States to have. Soon the Cold War was indeed a thing of the past and even more Pentagon and other US strategic analysis suggested that Cuba was no longer a threat.[4] In that light, conservatives and Cuban-Americans began to fear that such views would begin to affect US policy in ways that would open up cooperation between the two countries. In Congress, members attached what was to be known as the Graham Amendment (after Senator Bob Graham of Florida) to an appropriations bill in late 1997. The amendment ordered the Pentagon to report formally to Congress on whether Cuba was still a military threat to the United States. It asked as well for specific responses as to Cuba's nuclear, biological, and chemical weapons potential, the offensive capabilities of its forces, and potential subversion, terrorism, and narcotrafficking roles in which the island's armed forces were, or might become, engaged.

The report's findings were leaked to the press in March of the next year and immediately caused a storm in Miami. They were clear and said in no uncertain terms that in the view of the Department of Defense, Cuba was no longer a military threat to the United States and downplayed Cuban intentions and potential interest in nuclear, biological, or chemical weapons, that Cuba had no real offensive capabilities although it was capable of defending itself well, and that other issues were not major. The attacks on the report from "Miami" and its Congressional representatives became acerbic in the extreme and a shaken Secretary of Defense William Cohen sent the report back to the Pentagon for review. In April, the final document was sent to him but continued to argue that Cuba was no military threat to the United States.

A variety of US senior officers, mostly retired but all with considerable Latin American experience, defended the report and poohpoohed the extremists' concerns. Frequently extolling the virtues of the FAR and in some cases calling for working together with Cuba on common problems, they nonetheless felt, in the words of General Charles Wilhelm, one of those who helped prepare the report, that the FAR "has absolutely no capability to project itself beyond the borders of Cuba."[5]

This extraordinary situation, where the defense ministry of the country that has another country as its official "enemy" determines that the other country is not only not a threat but should also be worked with on defense and security issues, probably frightened the conservatives more than anything else. No one could accuse such officers, or the Pentagon itself, of being anything but keen on national defense. This courageous position of many members of the Department of Defense wishing to take another look at the Cuban issue persisted in Washington even in the George W. Bush presidency but was visible even at this early stage. And while it is of course the result of US thinking and analysis, it is also directly related to Raúl's policy of finding things for the FAR to do that would be useful to Washington and create such a constituency arguing with force for a Cuban relationship of a more positive nature. In a country with no money for new equipment much less naval shipping, Raúl's FAR had only laid down three patrol craft in the long and harsh years of the Special Period. All three had one objective: antidrugs and antinarcotics operations which, even if they fulfilled Cuban objectives as well, cannot fail to show dramatically that among the highest of the nation's defense priorities has been finding ways to cooperate with the United States. This continues to be policy to the present day.

The FAR was therefore proving a useful diplomatic tool indeed at a time of great stresses on the diplomatic front almost across the board. And the end of its significant presence in Central America and southern Africa also augured well for bridge building with the United States. The arrival of George W. Bush, however, made profiting from this evolving situation a complicated affair indeed and growing US and Cuban military desires to see progress made between them had to wait yet again. Cuba would thus have to develop its relations with current or recent US allies rather than with the superpower itself.

One of those calling was of course Venezuela, a country whose military links with the United States were second to few in the region until the late 1990s and some of which continue to this day.[6] After a failed coup against the formally democratic but corrupt government of Venezuelan president Carlos Andrés Pérez in 1992, an unknown army airborne lieutenant-colonel was jailed, then released, and finally visited Cuba in 1994. There, Hugo Chávez was met at the Havana airport by Fidel Castro. The two men developed a firm friendship that was to serve Cuba well in the long term and has continued to prosper under Raúl, despite his less demonstrable affection for Chávez, since 2006.

Chávez, who did not hide his admiration for Fidel, was elected in December 1998 to the presidency of Venezuela, and soon showed his keenness to enter into a mutually profitable relationship with the

Cuban state. It was seemingly a match made in heaven. Cuba was in serious trouble during the Special Period, especially on the issue of oil, and no one felt the lack more than the FAR. While Cuban production of that commodity was improving, local sources were of poor quality and highly limited in yield. Venezuela could help to resolve this problem and in doing so liberate scarce Cuban foreign currency assets for other priorities. But this was far from a one-way street.

Chávez was determined to take Venezuela out of the backwardness and poverty that it had known, despite its great oil wealth, for all its history. His "revolution" aimed at free education of the masses, eventually improved access to medical care for all Venezuelans, a diversification of the economy away from almost exclusive dependence on oil, and ease of access for all to immensely increased educational, cultural, and sporting opportunities. In almost all of these spheres, Cuba could be of considerable help. The spectacular success of Cuba in the medical field, nearly across the board but especially in the production of doctors and other medical workers, was a fact. Cuba had teachers as well in large numbers, willing and able to go to the hinterlands of Venezuela or to the poor neighborhoods of its cities, where few middle-class Venezuelan educators were willing to venture. Likewise, Cuba had music and sports instructors of high quality and in large numbers and the keenness of Caracas to enhance those areas of national culture was palpable. Cuba was being thrown a lifeline in many senses, but it was not to grab onto it as someone drowning but rather as someone who had much to give as well for the help received.[7]

Venezuelan conservatives were not impressed, and the strong links between the US armed forces and those of the South American republic were a useful means to keep pressure on Chávez to behave as they wished. Indeed, in April 2002, civilian elements and conservative generals staged a brief coup attempt against Chávez that worked in unseating him but was forced to allow him back in the face of massive popular unrest supported by much of the rest of the armed forces. Fidel was a great support to Chávez, by the latter's own admission, during these difficult moments.

The power of the conservatives in the forces was curbed following this and room was found for a very limited connection between the two militaries, coupled with a rather more developed one between elements of the two security services. There is little known about these links except that they are there and will probably remain so for some time. More will be said on this bilateral connection later on.

With the end in early 1990 of the Sandinista government in Nicaragua, little remained in the way of real Russian interest in connecting again with Cuba. And it must be said that there was likewise little interest in Cuba for connecting with Russia, especially after the Lourdes Intelligence establishment was closed in 2001. The humiliation of keeping open this facility had been great with Raúl asking Moscow for $ 1 billion a year for it after the end of the strategic connection and Russia only offering $200 million and even that only for a few years.[8] Very limited defense links were established, or rather reestablished, with China in the mid-1980s and with Vietnam more a model than a partner in defense affairs, it must be said that the FAR had not broken out of its isolation in the way the nation as a whole had done with its own diplomatic isolation. Cuba could now boast diplomatic relations with 177 countries and 108 diplomatic offices in Havana, thus shattering the decades-old attempt by the United States to isolate it. But the FAR had not shared in this breakthrough and remained isolated indeed.[9]

Its usual spunk, however, was not lost from sight. The arrival of yet another right-wing government in the United States, that of George W. Bush in 2001, reinforced the view in key circles that the country, whatever the cost, would have to start taking defense seriously again. When despite Cuba's offers to help in the struggle against international terror on September 11 of that year and its prompt assurance to the United States that Cuban territory, airspace, and waters would never be allowed to be used for attacks on the United States, Bush put Cuba on the list of states sponsoring terror and continued the strongest of attempts to unseat the Revolution, the need for reinforced national defense and an even firmer deterrence posture became even more obvious to nearly all those observing the situation.

Money for the subversion of the Cuban state became more than ever available and not only to Cuban-Americans, who were weakened greatly by their part in the scandalous abduction of the boy Elián González at the end of the 1990s, and their defiance of the US justice system's actions in that case. In what became known in Cuba as the "Plan Bush," the policy he accepted from a commission set up to examine where the United States should be moving on Cuba, the president said that no movement in the bilateral relationship could be achieved unless Cuba accepted that whatever reforms it undertook, it would be obliged to end up with a democratic system based on the northern model and an economic system of the liberal economy type.

The dilemma for courageous and independent dissidents in Cuba was that this meant that if they proposed the same things, it was inevitable that they would be seen as at best dupes of the United States and at worst actual traitors. Dissidence in Cuba, given US money available to support it, is already in many cases something of a business and lacks great credibility or even relevance in the island's body politic. But that does not mean that there are not honest and real dissidents in Cuba who do not take money from the United States and truly wish for real reform of their country. This sort of policy on the part of the United States, where once again in its history, Cuba must simply bow to Washington and accept that its future is what that capital directs, simply cuts the grass out from under any real democratic movement along western lines that might one day flourish in the country.

Raúl ordered the FAR and the country's other security forces, with the island under all this renewed and powerful pressure from the United States, to batten down the hatches and begin to put itself in better order. Though not having any real extra money to work with, things had improved a bit and some repair schemes for vital elements of the forces equipment stocks were arranged and paid for. Raúl likewise pushed for originality in the bringing up to date of some weapon systems that could be improved, notwithstanding that in the new era of the general and worldwide phenomenon known as the Revolution in Military Affairs, then thought by most defense analysts to be going on, it was really replacement that was needed and not just repair and minor adjustments.

Replacement of stocks was of course not a possibility for the FAR or the nation and making do remained the only way to go. But the Bush administration's unilateralism, attitude to torture, military solutions to problems, and negativism about international affairs in general led to a curious change in Cuba, as well. Youth, especially urban youth, had for long been seen as the potential Achilles' heel of the system. They were often disenchanted, not having known the good days before the Special Period but only the trials, shortages, lack of opportunities, and negativism of those long years. Additionally, while able to study and in good health, they felt that there were no outlets for their energy and success in those studies, since salaries were so low and irrelevant and careers in their fields were so often seen as dead ends. Especially in the cities, they were often in a deep malaise and saw no end in sight or reason to engage as part of the system. They sometimes, at least when they were blowing off steam, even considered that a US takeover would not be a bad thing because at least it would bring greater prosperity and an end to that malaise. Needless to say, with this sort of thinking, even though it only represented a minority, there were real problems with the nation-in-arms idea and for the Guerra de Todo el Pueblo strategy. Under Bush, however, without much prompting from the government or party, there appeared to have been a dramatic change in that thinking that had real impact on defense preparation.

Young people again tended to believe that there was a real threat from the United States, that President Bush might actually be tempted by an easy victory in the immediate south given that everywhere else he faced stagnation or defeat. While there are no figures for such assertions, conversations with people connected with the reserves say that there was an upsurge in voluntary attendance at reserve courses and firing-range practices. Among young people one still hears much about how there is no way out of the present poor situation, but a "US solution" is virtually never mentioned.

In this context, it was possible for Raúl to imagine having again, for the first time since before the Special Period, a large mobilization exercise, or indeed a series of them. This would be done against the backdrop of a potentially real threat from the United States, which would therefore provide proper urgency for such a practice of national defense. Some analysts felt that this was only now possible because the nation feared Bush adventurism, and whatever it felt about its own sufferings, no US-imposed future was acceptable to the vast majority of the population.

Thus began again, after almost two decades in abeyance, the Bastión series of exercises, with Bastión 2004 being the first of several for which planning was ordered; the objectives were to test the mobilization system after so many years of decline, find out where the problems with it were, and move on to fix them. The exercise was in that sense a great success. It not only took place, already a positive sign in a country that had suffered as Cuba had done in the previous decade and a half, but also the militia personnel, reservists, and others called up for the exercise turned out properly and in the hundreds of thousands. The equipment they ran and the weapons they carried were not going to impress NATO specialists, and indeed did not do so, but there they were, the nation in arms or a large part of it at least, and seemingly ready and willing to defend the nation and its political system.

Public military parades also began to take place with more frequency at this time. While they had never died out altogether, they were now once more in favor. In addition, the FAR started using the slightly more available supply of paper (the country could import virtually none during the lowest points of the Special Period) to reinforce the public mood in support of defense with a series of books and pamphlets on the military history of the island and of the Revolution. All manner of books came out not only on the campaigns of 1956 through 1959 but also of those of Máximo Gómez, Antonio Maceo, Ignacio Agramonte, and the impressive series of commanders and individuals that make Cuban military history so interesting. The emphasis was very much on patriotism and the deeds of the fallen of yesteryear; FAR writers could be seen everywhere, especially in the weekly book launches at the Palacio del Segundo Cabo (the administrative offices of the Spanish second-in-command on the island in colonial times) in Havana, presenting new volumes with their implicit and sometimes explicit call for today's youth to be worthy of the nation's heroes. Most of the modern works were part of Raúl's long-standing desire to have the military history of the revolutionary struggles studied and written down. In his view, this had not been done properly, and he repeatedly stated that the revolutionaries had been able to make history but not to write it.

Plans for Bastión 2006 continued with more emphasis on discovering errors and also on correcting those that had been discovered in the first of the renewed exercises. Raúl was busy indeed with a FAR fully engaged in directing a huge part, some said up to 60 percent, of the economy; producing a great deal of its agricultural harvest; deterring a potential invader; impressing on, at the same time, that possible aggressor that Cuba was a more useful potential partner than current enemy; providing support for MININT and other agencies that reported to the FAR's minister; continuing in charge of the constantly needed natural disaster response of the nation; engaging in the many social roles assigned with the Special Period; ensuring control of Cuba's skies, territory, and neighboring seas; and doing much else that it was ordered to undertake.

Then both the natural hurricane season and the potential political tempest of 2006 hit, putting an end to the idea of a full-blown Bastión 2006 and to any plans Raúl might still have harbored of his own personal retirement to a quieter family life. The major hurricane of that year hit the westernmost province of Pinar del Río just as the FAR was deploying, largely in the eastern parts of the country, to begin the exercise. Rare as such a situation is, the forces were thus not as poised as they usually are for the severe weather and the destruction that hit the west at that time. Rushing into action, however, with characteristic speed, they eventually mounted the relief operation with good success. The exercise would have to wait. But the potential political hurricane was to have much greater and longer lasting impact than the climatic one.

Chapter 6

A Military Man as President

With the illness of President Fidel Castro, announced on July 31, 2006, Raúl Castro was, as expected, named interim president and head of a small group that was to guide the country until Fidel resumed office. That day was not to come and Fidel resigned formally as head of state, although not as comandante en jefe, in February 2008, making way for Raúl's formal election as president in his own right at the end of that month. Raúl, who had by all accounts been looking forward some day to retirement and spending more time with his four children and eight grandchildren, once more took on added responsibilities rather than lesser ones because the Revolution needed him and his capacities at a difficult time.

The subject of this book is of course Raúl as an "other" kind of military leader to what is generally viewed as the Latin American type. And yet another Latin American military man arriving at the presidency must of course give any observer with knowledge of the region pause. But the nature of the first years of his presidency show that he has brought to government a leadership that is in many ways military in style even if he is far from being merely another Latin American military leader who has become head of a government.

Fidel of course has vast military experience as well as Raúl. It was Fidel who organized and led the Moncada expedition in which his younger brother served as a mere rifleman. It was he who was the center and director of the organization of the small group of men in prison after that adventure who were to be the soul of the Ejército Rebelde and in many senses of the revolutionary government as well when it came to power. It was equally he who over many months in Mexico organized and trained the tiny force that landed in Cuba in December 1956 to begin the serious and lengthy armed struggle

against Batista. He likewise was the commander of that armed insurrection and the key thinker and "doer" in making it successful in
capturing power in January 1959. And it was Fidel who gave the
leadership, inspiration, and organizational lead to the building of
the strategies and armed forces that would deter attack on Cuba for
decades, leading in the actual fighting to defend it in the Bay of Pigs
invasion of 1961 and taking a major role in directing Cuba's armed
struggle in Africa on various occasions.

Thus it would be absurd to suggest that there was a "civilian" president in Cuba before Raúl assumed power. Fidel was no such thing,
and it is clear that his status as comandante en jefe had real meaning
not only to him but to the citizens of his country, as well. The widely
used slogan *commandant en jefe, ordene* (commander in chief, order),
so reminiscent of Mussolini's Italy, was in a Cuba that was under
something quite akin to real siege, very much an audible expression
of the military reply to the need for national mobilization. The leader
of such a country in such a context had to have much of the soldier
in him in order to keep the system afloat and act as a visible symbol
and personification of the national will to defend the revolution and
deter any attackers.

That, however, is not the whole story. Fidel, while wearing a uniform most of the time, did not do so as a classic military commander.
Willing to take on direct military duties when needed, and very interested in military history and affairs in government and out, he did not
see himself as a classic "military man." He was the serving president
of an embattled island on whose shoulders rested much more than
mere military duties, although they quite often took precedence over
anything else he was doing. For it was his political project of bringing
deep, radical, and abiding reform to Cuba that inspired him and made
him disposed to don a uniform, both to get to a place where he could
effect such changes and in order then to defend them.

Fidel's interest in racial equality matters and issues of women's
rights, his deep (sometimes excessive) involvement in even the minutiae of medical advances, his passion for the peasantry and agrarian
reform—all these marked his life and political goals. Improvements
in military fields were a way of getting to these wider objectives and
allowing them to be protected, and did not have value in and of
themselves.

Raúl's brother was no stranger then to military issues, but he was
very much a stranger to the day-to-day concerns of military institutions of a professional stripe. He was a revolutionary soldier *tout court*
and power allowed him to some very limited extent to leave such cares

behind him. While publishing interesting thoughts in his book *Sobre temas militares*, and obviously having exceptionally poignant thinking about the military matters behind his campaign in the mountains and afterward in power, Fidel did not consider himself a particularly "military" thinker.[1] His "*Reflexiones*," published in the press since his retirement, have rarely touched Cuban defense matters, except in relation to what he sees as the continuing US threat to world peace, and have been much closer to his passionate inclinations toward foreign policy, medicine, and Cuba's place in the world as a result of its medical workers abroad, education, and other social issues.

It is the conclusion of this author that Raúl, on the other hand, is very much a military man, but not one of the traditional Latin American stripe. He is a *revolutionary* military man, but one who knows the worth both of military approaches to getting things done and of military values when seen at their best. And it is argued here that in government, even for the time in which he has so far exercised power, he has shown a remarkably 'military' way of going about business and a military style of government although most distinctly one shorn of the excesses of most such governments in the history of the region. Nonetheless that military style is present in everything he does and how he goes about doing it.

A first comment on this state of affairs is that it should not surprise us. It is no doubt true that he hated his time as a boy in military school, but most attempts at getting a better look at him seem to suggest that this reaction was more about compulsory prayer and meaningless discipline than about a rejection of things military or discipline per se. Indeed, everything we know about him after that school, his limited involvement in the party youth organization, training and preparing for the Granma expedition while in Mexico, soldiering and command in the Sierra, full commanding of the forces and running of the ministry, suggest that he knew very well the importance of discipline and could even be expected to apply it with vigor when needed. Some critics suggest that this application of vigor was on occasion excessive.

In a sense, Raúl has never known any life but the military. While Fidel trained to be a lawyer, practiced law until he was 25, and became organizer and head of a political movement that he then led in power from the age of 32, Raúl knew no such wider experience. It is true that he was active in politics, like his brother, at university in Havana and that he travelled with political objectives at that time. But he fought at the Moncada when he was only 22 and since then, until becoming president at the age of 77, has either been preparing for war, engaged in it, or commanding, organizing, and administering the armed forces that would do so.

He is likewise the only soldier in Cuban history to ever have 'general de ejército' rank, although Máximo Gómez, the Dominican former professional army officer who volunteered to fight with the Cuban rebels, and indeed command their insurrection, reached something of a similar rank during the wars for independence. Raúl has been in a military (or prison) uniform with primarily military responsibilities for at least (as of the date or writing) 55 years of the total of 60 years of his adult life so far and is frequently in uniform to this day even though in no way with such regularity as had been the practice when his brother was president.

Military Government or a
Military Style of Government?

The arrival of Raúl to power surprised no one in Cuba where his assumption of power, both pro tempore in 2006 and formally in 2008, was taken as a given. For nearly half a century Fidel had announced on any number of occasions that in case of his incapacitation, Raúl would be taking over until such time as the political process set up by the Constitution of the Republic decided on someone else.[2] In addition, ever since Fidel's first major trip to South and North America in 1959, it was normal for Raúl to be left in charge.

It was of course very different in Miami and other centers of extremist anti-Castro exiles where many hoped that Fidel's leaving power would lead immediately to some sort of popular uprising which would topple the socialist state and bring in some other system—the nature of which was uncertain. Such was their power in the press and government of the United States that they were able to make such a view that of the vast majority of those commenting on Cuba in that country, and such was the power of the United States and the influence of its "conventional wisdom" that those views were often virtually the only ones heard in Western Europe, Canada, and even farther afield.

The transfer of power on July 31, 2006, took place, however, without a single recorded incident of any kind on the island. There were no demonstrations and there was no increase in police presence, although there was a mobilization of some reserves and their deployment to the wartime posts they took whenever US attack was possible. There was not even the appearance of more graffiti on the walls of the country nor was there a single brick thrown at a public building. It simply could not have been a more routine passage of power or a less eventful end, as it was to prove to be, of an era.

What was not understood elsewhere was that any Cubans opposed to the Revolution who heard the shocking news of Fidel's illness and the nomination of Raúl that night knew that nothing could really be gained by their action in opposition to it. Those who backed the socialist experiment wanted a peaceful succession and had been expecting just such an event for decades. And visibly very few of those who did not like the experiment were willing to act to take advantage of one of its moments of crisis in order to try to get rid of it. They knew that opposition to any action they might take would be widespread and would include not only a loyal police, armed forces, and security apparatus but also hundreds of thousands or even millions of ordinary people. Civil war or at the very least bloody disorder would be the result, and from that could only come disaster and US intervention, as every Cuban child learns when taught about the nation's so often tragic nineteenth and twentieth century history.

Added to this is the fact that many Cubans, perhaps most, were neither fiercely in favor nor fiercely opposed to the socialist government or Fidel Castro. They hoped for better times than those they had been forced to live through for over a decade and a half, but they were clearly willing to give Raúl Castro the benefit of the doubt to bring those about through his actions and not through those of his enemies. They did not wake up the next morning with many other options, given the political context of Cuba and the generalized knowledge that civil war would be costly in blood and end inevitably with foreign occupation occurring yet again. As one Spanish security expert put it at the time, "*Esta vez si alguien va al monte, va solo*" (This time if anyone takes to the hills he does so alone).[3]

With few factors pushing for antigovernment action, and many pulling against it, no opposition of any kind actually surfaced, and Raúl drove to work in his normal vehicle cavalcade the next morning without incident and indeed to the applause of many in the streets.[4] While US and especially Miami radio and television produced story after story of military coups, Fidel and Raúl's assassinations, riots in the streets, cavalry charges against demonstrators, and the like, the Cuban government went on with business as usual in an atmosphere of absolute calm.

It was not, however, to be business as usual in another very important sense. For Raúl Castro is not Fidel Castro. He is a loving brother, a great and firm admirer, a loyal servant and minister at one time, a fellow combatant and junior officer at another time, and much else to

Fidel, but he is *not* Fidel. His style of government was not to be Fidel's, even though he came to power to serve the Revolution that Fidel had organized, led, and defended over more than a half-century.[5] If Raúl had not intended to spend his remaining years in the position in which he found himself, as most people who know him suggest, he did not show either positive or negative emotion at taking on the job or getting to work at it.

Historians of the future will have to work out, if they can, what he was actually thinking at that time. What we do know is what he said and what he did and that was to accept the nomination and get to work, in the quiet but effective way that he was so well-known for in the FAR, on keeping the Revolution going. At least two foreign military attachés in Cuba at the time remarked on how military this approach was, accepting quietly to do one's duty when the road ahead looked less than smooth.[6]

It was to be only one element of a military approach to much in his future government. It is not known whether Raúl expected Fidel to actually recover from his illness when he announced his temporary stepping down. The medical situation was, as the official announcement and Fidel's written statement said, a state secret as it had to be in Cuba's strategic context. But whether he already knew he would be staying for a long while or did not mattered little. His task was to ensure revolutionary survival, once again in his long public life, at a time when it was certain that counterrevolutionary forces would attempt to make the most of the of the comandante en jefe's poor health in order to overthrow the regime.

He got to work immediately to show that there was nothing unusual in this temporary succession situation and that the Revolution would be continuing its slow but relatively steady move out of the worst years of the Special Period. To the surprise of most press observers but not to most historians, the new president did not make a series of public statements, did not rush to the microphone to express his views, and did not give press conferences about the present or potential future situations. Instead he went to work each day, spoke in private or in small forums to ministers, senior officials, armed forces officers, and specialists on issues of importance, and began to make an even wider mark on the nation than that he had already done in his long career.

The exact details elude us for the present, but it is certain that in these discussions he made clear that his would be a government loyal to the principles of Fidel and Fidel's objectives in safeguarding the *logros de la Revolucion* (achievements of the Revolution) but that his style would not be the same. There would be no long speeches lasting late into the night. And there would be no even later meetings carrying on until near dawn as had become the routine with Fidel, especially when there was a major question at hand or an important foreign visitor in town. Ministers and other officials would be expected to conduct work days of normal length and be home in the evenings. Raúl would be expecting to do the same and would not be welcoming calls to change that routine unless they were truly urgent.[7]

Even more dramatically, the new acting president made clear that he would be conducting affairs in a way that any military officer would find as normal routine for a soldier. That is, those receiving orders from Raúl would know that they were being given a task after real study had been put into it beforehand, and after they had been asked where possible their views on it; they would be given timelines for completion and resources to achieve the task, and asked their views on those points, as well; then they would be sent off to do the job. They would not be micromanaged, nor brought in constantly to give progress reports, nor hassled from above in general while they got the job done. However, they would be strictly judged, an activity Raúl was already famous for within the FAR, for the quality of the product. If they had difficulties that they foresaw, they were to share them with Raúl before embarking on the task at hand. But once orders were given then it was up to the officials to carry on and do the work properly.

No military man could possibly find fault with this standard procedure for the affairs of persons in uniform. This was how, in essence, military administration was supposed to work. While of course there are micromanagers, bosses too prone to worry and to pass on their worries too early, and the like, in the defense forces of all countries as there are in other walks of life, it was this approach that was and is known as "military" in most parts of the world.

Of course, this was not how Fidel was known to operate and was a major change for the Cuban administration. Fidel is doubtless a brilliant man and has such prestige in the Cuban state and nation, more like a monarchical figure in many senses than a more republican head of state, that most simply stand in awe of him and received his orders without qualm. And the senior officials of the Cuban state had long become accustomed to a degree of micromanaging, which they might not have liked but which they had accepted as part of Fidel's characteristic way of doing business successfully.[8]

Late hours, long meetings called at virtually any hour, micromanagement throughout or at least very often during the carrying through of a task, little patience with doubters, the assumption of unquestioning obedience, a certain ad hockery in planning, sometimes insufficient study of the problem at hand before a solution was chosen—these are some of the criticisms, right or wrong, that have been made about Fidel's management technique.[9] This approach has without doubt, under his leadership, given some extraordinary results, and the survival of the Revolution against all odds is a clear indication that one should be wary of criticizing it too easily.

It may have best worked, however, only with Fidel's charisma, command presence, prestige, history, and brains, and may not be especially helpful as an approach to one missing any of those attributes. It is no slight to Raúl to suggest that his skill set and strengths are probably not those of Fidel; he has said as much himself.

He has often expressed the need for the institutionalization of the Revolution since the original leadership, and especially of course Fidel, cannot be expected to be around forever. On this point he has been as clear as he could possibly be. If the Revolution is to survive into the future, it must have institutions, procedures, and even mere approaches to doing things that are standard, known, and automatically applied, and that follow sound techniques and legitimate arrangements. If such things are not anchored now, it is pointless to imagine that, lacking leaders like Fidel, the Revolution can last long or best carry on. Even before he was formally elected by the *Asamblea Nacional* (National Assembly) to the presidency, Raúl asked for authority to change the very structure of government, cutting the number of ministries among other changes and calling for a sustained effort at truly institutionalizing the Revolution. He made his argument:

> Today we need a more compact and functional structure, with a smaller number of agencies of the central administration of the state and a better distribution of the functions they do. We have to make more efficient the management of our government. Institutionality, and I repeat the term "institutionality," is an important support of that decisive proposal and one of the pillars of the invulnerability of the Revolution in the political field, and so we must work for its constant improvement.[10]

Reformer or Conservative?

Early on in the new but still "temporary" government, Raúl commissioned a large number of studies by expert practitioners and academics on a wide range of subjects that he wished to understand better in order for him to be prepared to make decisions on where Cuba should go. These included above all major questions of economic policy in light of the slowing pace of recovery from the Special Period. All involved appear to feel that they were serious studies and not made in order to give the impression of change without any intention of actually having any to speak of.[11] And this brings us to the question of whether the president of Cuba is a reformer or a conservative and what this means in terms of his position as a military man.

Raúl is known in Cuba as being the man behind the rectificación process of the 1980s, and the main impetus to reform in the early 1990s when the Special Period broke upon Cuba. He is also a frequent spokesman for the need for change, perhaps most dramatically demonstrated in his acceptance speech to the Cuban people after his election as president de jure in February 2008. As a result of these stands, many excellent observers of the Cuban scene see him as a reformer.

Raúl is also known by some as the supposedly determined and dogmatic member of the Socialist Youth movement in 1953, the hard-hearted prosecutor in the first trial of a supposed counter-revolutionary as early as the training phase for the 1956 invasion in Mexico, a key figure in the harshness of the trials conducted by the Revolutionary Tribunals in the early months of the new government, an impediment to free academic discussion in the closing of the relatively free-thinking journal *Pensamiento Propio* in 1972, a stickler for heavy sentences in the Ochoa trials of 1989, and the main mover in the blocking of many elements of intellectual and cultural *apertura* in the mid-1990s, especially in the celebrated CEA Affair.[12] As a result of all this, and much more, many equally qualified observers see him as a conservative.

This study comes to the firm conclusion that he is neither and both. To explain, Raúl is a dedicated revolutionary who has given his whole working life to the Revolution and its goals of social justice and national independence. His reformism and his conservatism join on this hard bedrock of philosophical thought and action. If Raúl feels that reform is necessary for the efficiency and progress of the Revolution, and for the furtherance or protection of its main goals, he will be interested in reform. If he feels that reform is dangerous for the survival or well-being of those goals, he is interested in conservatism. This is visible throughout his lifetime, in both speeches and actions. But he reminded us of it in his speech at the July 26, 2007, celebrations in Camaguey, the first at which he spoke as president of Cuba and thus the first of the great occasions of state when he could make his views heard internationally and by the whole nation.[13] However, already by October 2006, when he had been in power for less than three months and was only an interim president, Raúl had encouraged open criticism of the things that did not work in the system and required reform, especially the monopoly exercised by the state on the purchase and sale of food, widespread fraud in the public sector, and generally poor services given to Cuban citizens across the board.[14]

What are these key logros that Raúl will feel obliged to maintain at virtually any cost? They include first and above all national independence, the long sought after objective of Cuban nationalism since the early nineteenth century, and a goal frustrated by endemic disunity, defeat in the early wars against Spain, US occupation on at least three occasions and excessive influence throughout the Republican period of 1902 through1958, and the lack of a truly national Cuba élite. In this he is of course joined by most Cubans but especially his own armed forces, the guarantors that this recently gained independence is not again lost. Nothing else in the revolutionary catechism rings out to Cubans like this question of national independence, so difficult to achieve and so hard to maintain in Cuba's geostrategic situation.

The second is surely related to Cuba's social context before the Revolution. Three things could bring ruin to a Cuban family before 1959. The first was attempting to send a son to school and university in order for him then to try to bring the whole family up by its bootstraps through his new social and professional position. The second was significant illness in the family, the costs of which could be ruinous to even fairly well-off people. And the third, less generalized, was proper burial for one's parents, a goal of all Cubans, in a country where that meant a good burial plot, a fine monument, a full funeral mass, a well-compensated priest, and something at least akin to a feast afterward for the family and friends of the deceased.

Fidel moved quickly to address the first two and with time even to tackle the third of these. Free and eventually paid education, to the level the student's intellectual attributes brought him or her, was soon the official goal of the Revolution and not long after a fact of Cuban life. A massive alphabetization program, the biggest and most successful in Latin American history, effectively put an end to illiteracy not only in the cities but even in the most rural zones of the nation. Cuba moved from two universities before the Revolution to almost 20. In addition, technical schools exploded in number and quality, and Cuban mass public education became what most specialists see as Latin America's finest. The impact on Cuban life has been simply exceptional and the cultural and intellectual life of the nation has never been the same.

Secondly, in the field of public health, Cuba has an imperfect but very good and absolutely universal health program for everyone, including visitors to the country. Its successes are simply exceptional by any standards, and by those of the rest of Latin American and the Third World in general, almost defy belief. There is no requirement for anyone on the island to put money aside to have access to this system, although it must be said that during the Special Period, the reinforced embargo and the generally depressed situation led to a weakening of public access to expensive drugs from abroad, and this is an issue with which many Cubans do have to deal.

Even in the less dramatic field of proper burials, the Revolution moved soon to provide a civilized system that would take the terrible psychological and financial burden off the family's shoulders alone. The state now provides the plot for a family's loved ones. It also ensures that the deceased will be brought from anywhere on the island for burial where he or she wished at no cost to the family. In addition, the stone for the burial, while hardly monumental or luxurious, is provided as is the general maintenance of the plot in the future. Transportation for the friends and family members of the deceased, by bus or even taxi, is also covered by the state.

Perhaps even more striking for a socialist, and for a long time even an atheist, state, the government also provides at its expense a priest for the mass and the chapel or related arrangements necessary for decent Christian burial. And when the ceremony is over, the state provides a decent if frugal reception for all who have attended the event. It is difficult to imagine any reform taking away these logros of the Revolution any time soon.

It is also difficult to think that several other planks of the revolutionary program will be done away with or even much weakened. The exceptional progress of women in the country, professionally especially but also to some degree in the home, is noted by almost all observers of the national and Latin American scene. Changing this state of affairs would be difficult in the extreme, and the trend is still in the other direction in a nation where *machismo* is very much an enduring feature of life.[15]

Progress with racial equality is also an achievement of exceptional value in Cuba over the years of the Revolution. Its weakening under the severe impact of the Special Period has brought major concerns to the government and to intellectual debate in society as a whole. But to undo its progress with changes of any kind, formal or informal, would be a blow to the Revolution that Fidel, who takes this issue particularly seriously, could not countenance. Rather it is likely that the state will use every means possible to shore up the progress made so far at a time where almost everyone studying the phenomenon of the resurgence of visible and audible racism agrees that it is indeed on the rise.

Aside from these issues, though, there seems to be much room to maneuver. It is a fact that Raúl has moved into some of those areas with drive in recent years and shown that he is not the excessively dogmatic communist that some have made him out to be for over 50 years. He has shown himself willing to listen to quite radical reforms if they do not appear to be likely to hurt these central logros and to be adamant in opposing those that might well bring about distinctly negative change that would endanger them or the wider central elements of *comunismo con una cara humana* (communism with a human face), as his brother envisaged it.

Some previously unthinkable points in the socialist canon have been jettisoned when they did not meet the needs of Cuba as it faces current challenges. For instance, Raúl has understood from his military background and the situation in industries run by the FAR that remuneration in economic terms is often vital for success in production and that volunteer labor, while never to be thrown out entirely, has its very distinct and important practical limits. He has also agreed to the abandonment of a central tenet in accepting that the idea of "to each according to his needs and from each according to his abilities" has to be nuanced in order to keep an economy on track and that this precept has to be seen as an eventual goal and not yet in any way a feasible reality. Connected to this, one has seen that production-related pay is now common in much, if far from all, the Cuban economy with not only employees who work more effectively getting better salaries but also with inefficient workers actually receiving worse ones. This was unimaginable before recent reforms.

Raúl has also shown a refreshing willingness to take new paths in the nearly sacred area of collective farming with many thousands of farmers of late receiving plots of land from the state, which are theirs in many senses and much freer from bureaucratic red-tape in their functioning than other parts of the agricultural production sectors. It is, however, still to be seen how well this works out in the end especially if the thorny issue of credits for seed, machinery and clearing the land is not available in sufficient quantities.

On the wider political front, Raúl has not only allowed debate to widen in Cuba in the public sphere but has also actually called for it to happen. Two wide-ranging public debates about what Cubans wish to see in the future took place in the first two years of his presidency, and the level of discussion on major topics of current interest in forums such as the *Ultimo Jueves* public sessions, the journal *Temas*, or the newspapers *Juventud Rebelde* or *La Calle del Medio*, to name but a few, firmly counters the idea that Cubans are not allowed to have opinions or to express them in public. Even more dramatically, in his major policy speech of January 2012 at the end of that year's Party Congress, Raul spent a full six minutes of the 23-minute speech speaking about the need for Cubans to debate how best to improve the Cuban model of democracy, calling for this process to begin with the democratization of the party, and accepting implicitly that there was much work to be done in making such a Cuban democracy modern. In the Cuban system, this means that public debate on the subject is now permitted, and in some senses, actually encouraged.

This does not of course mean that Cuba has as yet a free press or freedom of speech. But it does mean that to not recognize the changes already occurring in the last years of Fidel's rule and the first half-decade of Raúl's is to miss what is happening in Cuba in an extremely important sphere. As elsewhere, revolutionary discipline is still imposed in order to defend the Revolution from its enemies but within that discipline, much discussion is not only permitted but also encouraged from the top.[16] This could not be any closer to the best traditions of military life in the world's most impressive armed services.

There are many other logros of the Revolution that, however appealing, may be abandoned in the future without a major disruption of the quality of life in Cuba and which might be reinstated later when the country comes out of the present deep crisis. One thinks of some obvious ones. Mass access to sport is now a given in Cuba. Gone are the days of expensive events beyond the range of the average Cuban. Revolutionary sport is noncapitalist in the sense firstly that pay is not related to television visibility, advertising on uniforms, or style or effectiveness of play, and secondly that it is not meant to be a moneymaker for the team, state, or even, in the socialist egalitarian sense, the individual player.

Instead it is about enjoyment and quality of play overall. Everyone in Cuba has access to the most important sports events of the year for one or two pesos (about four to eight US cents). If there is interest in attending an event, it is hard to argue that there is any obstacle for anyone's doing so. Is this a logro of the Revolution that is untouchable? With Fidel's love for sport and the sports-mad nature of so much of the Cuban population, it might on many scores be sad to see this system go. But if Raúl decided to do so, it could surely be abandoned without irreparable harm done to the main thrust of Cuban socialism.

Access to the arts and culture might cause more debate. Here again a Cuban pays 5 to 10 pesos (roughly 20 to 40 US cents) for the best seat in the opera, ballet, concert hall, or theatre and one or 2 pesos (4 to 8 cents) for the cinema. There is absolute ease of public attendance at such events as a result. There is likewise little doubt that this is a real logro of the Revolution and has stimulated, with the rest of Cuba's huge system of supporting the arts in general, the explosion of the cultural scene in the country since 1959. If the state needed to reform these arrangements, it is difficult to imagine more capitalist approaches in this field as any sort of death-knell for Cuban socialism.

Housing is a more difficult area of course, as it has been in Cuba since colonial times, and so is private property in general. But even in these more problematical areas of life and socialism's approach to life, there may be more room to maneuver than is at first seen. In any case, it is too early to say what might be reformed and what might not be without undue damage done to the socialist system of which Raúl and his fellow revolutionaries are so proud.

The main point remains that Raúl has been found to be a reformer when he believes that it is time for reform of the Revolution in order to move forward, and has been found to be a conservative when it is time to dig in and hold the line in the face of threats to the survival of the Revolution. In the view of this author, this should not surprise us, and once again it is quite in keeping with military traditions as to how to address questions of change. It is worth remembering that one of the strongest expressions of conservative military thought is "When there's no need to change, there is need not to change," and that the other side of that military coin is the equally powerful idea that "Tradition is a wonderful servant but a terrible master." While both those expressions come from British and not Latin American experience in military spheres, Latin American militaries are perfectly comfortable with the thought process they represent. Finding the proper balance here as elsewhere is the challenge.

It is important to not lose our way in this discussion. Raúl Castro is the brother of Fidel, a member of the closest group around that leader for nearly 60 years, and a central figure of the Revolution and the revolutionary experiment. Leaving pedantry about 1953 aside, he is also a founder of the 26 de Julio movement, the closest of Fidel's collaborators in the long struggle to anchor the Revolution safely, a revolutionary thinker and at least sympathetic to Marxism from his early years, and part and parcel of the direction of this experiment for his whole political life. It is, to say the least, unlikely that he sees himself as someone who wishes to dismantle that Revolution or even see it severed in any serious way from its roots or its initial objectives. In that sense, he must be seen as at the most basic level a conservative on the issue of reform of what has been achieved so far. This may be Fidel's revolution first and foremost, but it is also, in the most profound sense, Raúl's.

At the same time, this military officer has learned in a long life of service that change is part of life, that nothing is permanent, and that to achieve things, or even to hold on to those things one has achieved, compromise on some matters may be necessary. Raúl has already shown that he can be in favor of quite major change if it results in the further shoring up of the key achievements of the Revolution. There is no reason as yet to think that his acceptance of necessary change has reached its limits. His speeches since 2006 have been full of the need for change in approaches to the defense of socialism and to its further flourishing, and to date his reforms have cut deep and been profound.[17] These points are surely the backdrop to any debate as to what extent he is a conservative or reformer. He is both and neither. Rather he believes in what is best for the Revolution, and if that means change so be it, and if it means no change so be it as well. Once again, the military is rarely uncomfortable with such realistic but still anchored ethical considerations.

It is useful at this time to give an overview of the reforms to date announced, implemented, or begun by Raúl's government as a way to give substance to the above discussion. For in these reforms, both in their scope and originality (in the Cuban context), can be found a great deal about the man and where he feels, after the careful study of issues to which he is so wed, Cuba must go.[18]

In July 2007, almost a full year into his de facto rule, Raúl termed the state milk collection and distribution system "absurd" and said that farmers could henceforth deliver the product directly to the consumers in their locality. And he issued his now famous statement, "To have more, we have to begin by producing more, with a sense of rationality and efficiency. To reach these goals, the necessary structural and conceptual changes will have to be introduced." The very next month, he ordered all state companies to apply the *perfeccionamiento* system, which the FAR had been implementing for several years, and to which reference has been made above, in order to improve production through the use of management techniques usually of a capitalist nature.

In the speech cited above on the occasion of his formal election to the presidency in February 2008, he said, "We must make efforts to find the ways and means to remove any deterrent to productive forces. In many respects, local initiative can be effective and viable." The message, while not surprising to many Cubans in the know about their new leader's approach, was still exceptional in the Cuban context. He spoke also in that address of the need to immediately face problems that urgently need reform while warning that deeper structural problems would take more time to resolve.

In the very next month came the sale to Cubans of previously forbidden or tightly controlled cell phones, computers, DVD players, and electric appliances as well as the lifting of bans on Cubans hiring cars and staying in hotels that had been limited to foreigners for most of the Special Period. At the same time began the major reform of the agricultural sector which has attracted so much attention in foreign and Cuban circles. Decentralization of decision-making in agriculture and the end of bureaucratic favoring of state farms over private establishments were ordered. And hikes in the prices paid farmers for their products were announced, the leasing of state land that was fallow was permitted, and the relaxation of many bureaucratic regulations that often hamstrung farmers' flexibility, especially in the area of direct sales to consumers instead of the state, was begun.

In August of 2008, after a further year of relatively few new changes being undertaken, Raúl began a major labor reform, which among other things linked wages to productivity at the individual level and not the corporate, and ended caps on personal earnings. In the fields of goods transport, there was a decentralization down to the municipal level; this also occurred in the important field housing construction.

The month after the March 2009 purges of the economics ministries saw savage cuts in the budget and imports, and plans were brought forward to stimulate mostly private farming in suburban areas around most of the country's cities. And over the summer, discussion ranged from further development of small businesses to the elimination of subsidies in some areas, with Raúl insisting on the striking statement that "ideas chart the course, the reality of figures is decisive," a statement Marc Frank of Reuters said was "ground-breaking...in a nation where ideology and politics trump economics."[19]

An office of the comptroller general of the Republic was likewise established by Raúl with a view to improving "economic discipline" and helping in the fight against corruption, the further relaxation of controls on roadside sales of farmers' products was made, and Raúl called for the "elimination of free services and improper subsidies...with the exception of those called for in the constitution." These last are those related to the national health service, education, and social security. In the following months, some industries experimented with the replacement of workers' free snack and lunch arrangements by a daily cash stipend for such expenses, and many licenses were issued to food vendors in cities across the nation.

In January 2010, taxi drivers began to benefit from a new scheme that would allow them to lease their cabs instead of receiving their very small state salaries for doing their work. Home construction and improvement regulations were also relaxed, and barbershops and beauty salons could henceforth be leased by those who worked in them rather than operated as part of a state-owned and run business.

During the year, decentralization of supply markets was also announced and the sale of construction materials to the public made easier. Holders of small garden plots were allowed to sell produce directly to the public at roadside stands. And rules for foreign holdings in tourism and leisure fields were also loosened somewhat.

Most dramatic of all was the decision in September 2010 to cut the state labor force by some five hundred thousand workers over a period of six months, a huge number for an island of just over 11 million people. This risky move sent shock waves through Cuban society like no other reform announced so far. On the one hand, it signals the seriousness with which Raúl and his government take the current crisis and the need to leave it behind through grasping the nettle of real reform, something with which the bulk of the people is clearly in agreement. On the other, it cuts deep and creates great uncertainty among much of the population at a time when things are not all that good in any case and where while the need for deep reform is acknowledged widely, the desire not to be hurt by it is generalized.

Accompanying the layoffs was the issue of 250,000 new licenses for self-employment in approved areas. Taxes were also changed while the rules for self-employment were loosened in important ways. Family businesses were at the same time authorized to hire labor and rent spaces in arrangements not seen on the island since before the socialist reforms of the 1960s. In fact, it has not proven possible to move as quickly with these lay-offs. But their message is clear and unsettling to many in a population accustomed to cradle-to-grave arrangements, one of which being guaranteed employment at however small a salary.

In 2011, many more reforms were announced and/or implemented. Listing them would prove impossible, but it is worth mentioning the beginning of modest credit arrangements for repairs to housing (often linked to setting up some sort of small business at home), for small businesses themselves, and for farmers with now greater plots who require seed, transport, and machinery for farming. The available funds so far have not been massive, but it is clear that the government sees such credit as central to any real recovery, particularly in the agricultural sector.

Also of note has been allowing for the first-time farmers to sell directly to hotels and other enterprises, the deep change represented by Cubans being allowed to buy and sell cars essentially without state controls, and new arrangements permitting the free purchase and sale of houses. Combined with the political reform called for by Raul, the first of its kind in many decades, change is more than in the air.

With all this, the previous talk of the slowness in the implementation of reforms under the new government, both on the island and off it, has nearly disappeared as observers and those most directly affected by the changes came to grasp their breadth and impact. Things were and are changing in Cuba and increased production has been and is the new byword. The road is still distinctly rocky with some areas of production showing good and steady growth while others seem to still stagnate.

The FAR and the New President

There is much talk in the United States media about a military takeover of the Cuban state, Revolution, society, and economy. And there is no doubt that with their minister of almost half a century now as head of state, the FAR has an assurance that defense matters will be attended to in a serious and effective manner. It is also true that the armed forces have probably almost as great a role in the running of today's Cuba as they had in the exciting but not very efficient days of 1959/60. The FAR provides ministers, economists, managers, teachers, doctors, nurses, professors, disaster relief specialists, bureaucrats, diplomatic servants, and of course sailors, soldiers, and airmen to the Revolution. The institution has its hands in all sorts of affairs often very far removed from the traditional roles of such forces. And Raúl has promised that the FAR will be better housed, equipped, armed, and treated in the future as part of a revamped and reinforced deterrent posture as Cuba comes out of the Special Period. This situation was perhaps best underscored by the major military parade held on

Armed Forces Day in December 2006, when newly refurbished if not particularly new equipment was brought out on display in the biggest parade since the Special Period began.

The suggestion that there has been a takeover, however, shows little understanding of how the Cuban state functions or indeed of what it is. The forces can simply not be seen in the usual Latin American sense or indeed traditional sense of any region. They are *revolutionary* armed forces, avowedly and proudly "political" and very much the servants of society and the state, as we have seen, in whatever tasks are set upon them, nontraditional as they may often be. The public in Cuba is entirely accustomed to seeing them in all manner of jobs, including economic, and has been so for a great many years.

There is no doubt that the public perception of the FAR is that its role in the country has grown significantly over the years of the Special Period. But this neither surprises Cubans, given the circumstances, nor does it necessarily trouble them unduly. In fact the usual reaction to the forces taking over a firm or an activity is along the lines of *"Bueno, por lo menos sabemos que de ahora en adelante funcionará"* (Well, at least we know that from now on it will work).

Despite the strains on the FAR over these years, it has also been a time of great excitement. Its central role in the country has never been clearer. The FAR has no doubt about its prestige among the public. Its own man is president and he knows the organization well and knows how best to use it. And if the forces are now much smaller and much less well-funded than in the past, they are nonetheless professional and even to some extent relatively well off when seen alongside the public at large. Problems abound, but as discussed before, morale is unquestionably high and the FAR's reputation can be summed up in the words of former diplomat and historian Carlos Alzugaray:

> The FAR, alongside its important sister institution, the Ministry of the Interior, constitute the most efficient and prestigious of the institutions created by the historic leadership of the country. Its popular origin, its constant linkage with the problems of the population, its historic contribution to the defence of the country and the liberation of other peoples, and its economic preparation, have meant that it enjoys the significant confidence of wide sectors of society. The higher officers of the armed forces accumulate a tradition of heroism, economic pragmatism, solvency and professionalism very unusual in Latin America, the Caribbean and the world.[20]

Specifically, the forces have seen their budgets recover to some extent, although they are expressed of course still in terms of a peso that has little value when compared to the years before the Special Period. On the equipment front, they have begun to improve conditions with the arrival of Chinese soft-skinned vehicles, especially jeeps and trucks. And some Russian spare parts have been purchased when hard currency has been available. Even some repairs of key systems have been possible. But weapons purchases have been something else altogether, with no new purchases of importance made and the FAR being asked to use ingenuity more than funds to keep defenses up. Potential suppliers such as China and Russia are also wary of too close a defense connection with Cuba because of potential US negative reactions to such links, even today. Washington is already troubled by what it views as Beijing's "penetration" of the whole region and especially the approaches to the Panama Canal, and China does not wish so close a link with Cuba as to raise even greater US suspicions.[21] In addition, the Chinese preference and often insistence is to be paid in cash, and although some barter arrangements have been made, that general issue is always there in Cuban-Chinese commercial transactions and doubtless also acts as a break on a further connection.

In the case of Russia, there are sometimes comments in Moscow about the return to a policy posture that includes Cuba as a friendly nation, and it is true that Russia has sold some spare parts to Cuba for the FAR and has spoken of a desire for a growing role in Latin America as a whole. But Moscow will probably continue to wish occasionally to play the "Cuba card" to show Washington it still has to some extent that option in its hand, while refraining from raising real concerns in the United States that it has intentions that include having a new and important defense relationship with the island. Cuba is also wary of such connections as it seeks to make progress in the bilateral relationship with its giant neighbor. The Russian squadron that trained with the Venezuelan Navy in 2009 stopped in Havana Harbor on its way home, but little actual connection was made between the two navies. Indeed, a recent article in *Granma* extolling the importance of the bilateral relationship did not even mention defense cooperation in its list of activities being jointly undertaken.[22]

Further to the subject of armed forces cooperation with other countries, Raúl has not succeeded in building such links with other forces either since the collapse of the Soviet bloc. The only connections of any importance at all have been with Venezuela, and even there the military relationship is not very developed and in only a small way reflects the impressive political and economic linkages the two nations have enjoyed since Hugo Chávez came to power in 1998.

The two armed forces are so different that it has not been at all clear how such closer links could be easily forged.

The Venezuelan military is accustomed to the very best in equipment and weaponry with money traditionally of relatively little importance in their acquisition. The air force flies very modern aircraft of sophisticated types with interceptors, light bombers, helicopters, and reconnaissance aircraft bought from Russia and Western European countries as well as the United States. In the navy, there are likewise mostly Western European ships, which have blue-water capabilities, at least in theory; these also tend to be very modern by Latin American standards. The army reflects the same pattern with modern artillery, armor, armored personnel carriers, reconnaissance vehicles, and the rest of the normal vehicles of a modern inventory, although with fighting vehicles largely of the lighter sort.[23]

Thus the FAR, despite its impressive history, is not in the same league as the Venezuelans in terms of modernity or sophistication of material. Further to this, the FAR can be forgiven for feeling that it does not have much to learn from its new friends, whatever the latter's financial situation. With enormous and successful combat experience in several parts of the world, a proven record of deterrence capacity, a successful reserve system unquestionably the best in Latin America, and very close to a real nation in arms, it is not obvious to Cuban officers what they have in common with forces that have not fought a war since 1830, remain surprisingly tied to United States doctrine and ways of going about business, and in general are not known in Latin American military circles for much sense of actual military urgency in their preparation for any real defense roles.

The Venezuelans have beefed up their military presence in Havana at the diplomatic level, going from a single defense attaché to one for each of the three services and a senior one who commands the group. And there are a few officers from the Venezuelan armed forces who attend Cuban staff college and other courses. There has also been great interest in Venezuela in learning about Cuba's exceptionally successful natural disaster preparation and relief arrangements which, as we have seen, are in great part a FAR responsibility. In this regard, Venezuela has deployed mixed armed forces/civil defense teams (called *brigadas* or brigades) to watch exercises in Cuba; these teams have even gone there for the real thing when hurricanes have struck the island. But it is easy to exaggerate the state of the defense relationship between the two countries as it now stands.

The politics of the relationship do not help either. Despite close relations at the bilateral level and multilateral connections of many kinds through ALBA or the *Alianza Boliviariana de los Pueblos de Nuestra America* (Bolivarean Alliance of the Peoples of Our America), the Cubans do not want, nor do they feel they need, an alliance or anything like it with Caracas. Such a firm arrangement, especially if it included collective defense commitments, is not tempting to Havana when it is trying to show the United States that it is not only not a problem but indeed is a potential help in dealing with that superpower's security and defense problems. Nor is the connection with Cuba without political costs at home for Chávez.[24] When President Chávez has called for a specifically anti-American alliance, Cuba has always been more than cool to the idea knowing well that it will raise alarm bells in Washington that Cuba does not need raised. For little gain in security terms, Cuba would be annoying the United States and suggesting that those in that country who see the Cuba-Venezuela connection as a defense problem, or even as an outright threat, are in the right. This is something that Cuba works quite hard to avoid.

Indeed, the surprise is that the one country with which Cuba has a truly growing and at least relatively impressive defense "relationship" is the United States, *el enemigo* (the enemy) to Cuba and a country that not only considers Cuba an enemy as well, but also has it on its list of 14 countries that sponsor terrorism and has by law a commitment to destroy its political, social, and economic system. The two countries' armed forces, and even their wider security forces, especially their coast guards, have developed links that surprise many, although neither side talks much about them for domestic political reasons.

There are monthly meetings of commanders of the Guantánamo US naval base and the *Tropas Guarda Fonteras* (Border Guard Troops or TGF) brigade that surrounds it in eastern Cuba, and those meetings can be called by either side via direct communications at any time if either party feels the need. The two sides have conducted military fire brigade exercises jointly to test their potential for bilateral cooperation in case of a fire. When the United States needed more Cuban airspace for the required air approaches to land aircraft safely at the base, the request was quickly granted by the Cubans. And when the United States decided to keep detainees from the Afghanistan and other antiterrorist missions on the base and built a large complex for the purpose, Cuba, as part of a policy of support for the United States in the aftermath of the September 11 attacks, offered to provide any extra requirements the base had.

The *Marina de Guerra Revolucionaria* (Revolutionary Navy) has even closer links, either directly or through the TGF, with the United

States. As we have noted, the Navy and TGF have as perhaps their most important day-to-day task to act against illegal migration from the island to the north, a job for which the US security forces have expressed their admiration and gratitude. There is since the mid-1990s *Crisis de los Balseros* (the crisis caused by the massive arrival of people from Cuba on rafts and other unsafe means) an accord with Washington to cooperate in immigration matters since, despite a formal policy of welcoming those "fleeing communism" based in the 1966 Cuban Adjustment Act, in reality the United States wants as few Cuban immigrants as possible.

Thus, Cuban action pleases the United States and the latter's policy of effectively not welcoming large numbers of illegally exiting Cubans pleases Havana. Naval craft and aircraft can be seen cooperating in implementing this reasonably joint approach. It has not been possible, however, for Cuba to convince the United States of the value of a similar accord on antinarcotics cooperation. While the DEA, US Coast Guard, and Pentagon make no secret of how much they would like such an agreement, the domestic political realities of southern Florida have so far precluded such an opening up in this field.

Here too, nonetheless, cooperation flourishes indirectly and directly. It does so indirectly in the sense that the British have had for some years a large, and the French, a small, program of assistance to MININT in this field. London is particularly happy with the results and says so repeatedly.[25] And it is an open secret that US security forces dealing with drug issues are privately very pleased with it as well as it is extensive and trains a good many Cubans to take part in antidrug operations with more efficiency and with better equipment. British and French warships have visited Cuba on numerous occasions to cement this connection, and the passage of valuable information between the various countries in this regard informally includes the United States, the main destination for the illegal drugs, as one might expect.[26]

Indeed, the United States, to the surprise of many, maintains a full-time United States Coast Guard (USCG) lieutenant-commander in Havana at the US Interests Section to ensure the smooth running of Cuban-US cooperation in the illegal immigration field, and he is not averse to keeping an eye out for valuable information in wider fields of joint endeavor. It is interesting to note that to date the United States has obviously been taking seriously the connection because the quality of officers chosen for this post has been very high indeed. Cooperation is *sistemático y fluído* (systematic and fluid) with the 7th District of the USCG in the most vulnerable zones of the southern United States and its approaches.[27]

Many members of both countries' security forces speak of confidence building taking place in this regard and of these activities as falling into the realm of confidence-building measures between the two countries. But it is difficult for the United States to be visibly indebted to Cuba for anything while it still treats it as an enemy and a pariah state. And it is almost as hard for Cuba to say publicly that it cooperates happily with the United States, "the enemy" in constant Cuban discourse, at this level. However, several Cuban publications have on occasion mentioned the fact and FAR and MININT officers are well aware that it is going on. It is also noteworthy that US agencies at the highest level have periodically complimented Cuba for its efforts.[28] Such praise was repeated as recently as early 2012 from the same sources.

Raúl has overseen the construction of these links with care. In foreign policy terms, this may well be the most important contribution the FAR makes as it helps build, if not a pro-Cuban constituency within US government circles, at least one that is prepared to see Cuba as a valuable partner in areas of serious security concern for Washington. These people, who are numerous in the Pentagon, DEA, coast guard, and immigration services, cannot be accused of being "soft on communism" or anything else, and yet they argue for cooperation with Cuba in areas of US and Cuban mutual security interest. This cannot be a bad thing for Cuba.[29] And Raúl must see it as such, or it would certainly not be happening.

The new president lost no time, either on becoming acting head of state or when he was elected formally to that position, in inviting the United States to turn the page on the hostile relationship of the last half-century. From his very first speeches as president, he insisted on the possibility of this happening. But as in the past, he made clear that Cuba would only negotiate a new relationship on the basis of mutual respect and equality of status and that there would be no question of simply giving in to the pretensions of the United States in terms of regime change or that country's dictating yet again Cuba's future along the lines of those mentioned in the various documents issued in the United States during the years of the most recent Bush presidency. This invitation was issued again, along with the equality and mutual respect points, by Raúl when President Obama was elected. And while there has not been any real reaction from the United States to the invitation and indeed in some ways, such as the tightening of travel regulations regarding countries that sponsor terrorism, the relationship has worsened, it is clear that Obama is at least slightly more open to the idea of dialogue with Raúl than Bush was with Fidel. It is too early to say where this might lead, but the existence within US security services of what is certainly a large number of senior people who strongly believe that it is time to bury the hatchet and take advantage of Cuba's disposition to assist in major US areas of concern could help to make progress possible over the longer term.[30]

Thus the FAR is now perhaps more central to foreign policy, more crucial to the functioning of the state and the economy, and closer to the head of state than it has ever been. Its professionalism is unquestioned; its loyalty is the same. Raúl can be happy indeed to have been able to face the tensions of political succession and some limited elements of overall transition with a force of such quality. And while it is doubtless true that the FAR's combat strength is not what it used to be, it would be very wrong indeed to count the FAR out. The combination of the regular force and reserves is still a daunting one for anyone considering attacking the country. And even though equipment is usually old, weapons are out of date, and many vehicles have been cannibalized, that does not mean there is not plenty of fight still in the FAR. High morale, determination, professionalism, and a sense of fighting for a cause like national defense are real factors in war, and the FAR has all of the above. So far US analyses show that the Pentagon understands this state of affairs perfectly well.

More Militarization and the Cabinet of Late Winter 2009?

In March 2009, one year after his election as president, Raúl sacked his foreign minister, economics minister, and several other ministers and senior officials associated with the management of the economy in previous years. Speculation was (and is) rife about what actually happened and why. And as with so many other political events in Cuba, precious little is actually known about the details outside the cúpula itself. Both Carlos Lage, economics minister, and Foreign Minister Felipe Pérez Roque were respected and well-known figures being tagged for some years as potential successors first to Fidel and then to Raúl. Little wonder then that there was so much surprised reaction to their dismissal. As with the Ochoa Affair 20 years before, this author believes it unhelpful to be reductionist about interpreting these events and changes. There are a number of factors involved here, and it is useful to mention all of them as they probably reflect on Raúl, his style of government, and where he wished to go as of that time.

The first factor to keep in mind is that Raúl had already been president for nearly three years and with very few exceptions still had a cabinet that was made up of his brother's appointees. While this was normal enough when there was some chance of Fidel's return to power, as time moved on, it became more and more strange for a leader known for being an excellent judge of character and competence and for being surrounded by people of his own choosing. Thus it is probable that the wish to have his own people in place in ministries as vital as those of foreign affairs and those related to his principal daily concern, the economy, was a powerful one in this choice of deep changes in the makeup of the directing team of the country.

It is also likely that the very fact that the foreign press and so many other observers of Cuba spoke so often and with such assurance of either Pérez Roque or Lage being probable successors sat ill with Raúl, as that sort of talk does with most rulers not ready to hand over power yet. Raúl has a great many things he clearly wishes to get done before he considers standing down as president, and constant naming of these men as potential successors must have been as annoying to him as they doubtless were to Fidel in his time.

There is also distinctly the issue of their indiscretion in the well-known incidents where they spoke dismissively of leaders of the government and of policies put in place by those leaders; additionally, they took improper liberties when speaking in places where they should have been more careful of the possible activities of foreign intelligence services. These situations may well have been what pushed Raúl to act, as so many observers have suggested, but there was more to it than just that. Certainly they were not seen as Raúl's type of men in the drive for greater institutionalization. As Carlos Alzugaray points out, linking the institutionalization effort and the dismissed officials:

> This is a matter of particular importance given the malaise accumulated with the effects of bureaucratism, inefficiency and cases of corruption. As has been shown by the dismissal of leaders of the highest level in March 2009, the excessive discretionality of staff and leadership in an environment of weakened institutions, is a breeding ground for the practice of influence peddling and double standards.[31]

It may also be possible that Pérez Roque, and to some extent Lage, were around too long and were too well-known (and easily quotable) for anti-US statements than Raúl wanted for the people he hoped would be available for real and potentially positive negotiations with the United States in the future. Anyone in those posts in the Cuban government over such a long time would have been obliged to make many statements about the United States that were far from flattering, but the very length of their stay in the cabinet, especially in the case of Lage, and the nature of the terrible bilateral relationship over that period, ensured that they were known as shrill critics of Washington in many sectors in the United States. But this is mere conjecture.

Less so is the possibility that Raúl wanted to signal his seriousness about the economy by showing that those closest to former policies were no longer needed and that a new team would now tackle economic issues of vital importance to the country. While it was known that Lage was something of a reformer himself, here we were to have a new team very much of Raúl's choosing, much as was his approach to running the Ministerio de las Fuerzas Armadas. That team was personally loyal to the new president, and had risen under his wing and been appointed by him. Whatever direction Raúl might choose, toward reform or retrenchment, it could be counted upon to be faithful to him and loyally support the choices he made.

This raises another fundamental element of his leadership style and points to one more area of a very military basis to it. Antoine Henri de Jomini, the great Swiss strategist, with Karl von Clausewitz, his Prussian counterpart, surely the most important military thinkers of the nineteenth century, put the matter clearly when they wrote that the most important thing for a monarch, a statesman, or a general to be able to do well was choose his subordinates, including especially his successor in case of need.[32] This has been a marking element of Raúl's success. As we have seen, for the Segundo Frente's departure in March 1958, Fidel gave him a list of 100 men from whom he chose 50 for his epic task. He then had many moments when the choice of the right man for the job was essential for combat efficiency reasons. Then early on, as minister and commander in Oriente, he had a great many such decisions on people to make. Subsequently, for the defense of the Revolution against internal and external foes, and for the protection of his brother against the huge number of assassination attempts aimed at him, he had to choose the right people. For operations abroad, the same requirement for his decision-making on people was there. The 'internationalist' operations the FAR engaged in around the Third World in support of "progressive" forces in Africa, Asia, and Latin America, complicated at the best of times both militarily and politically, continued to test his ability to make choices about people and their fitness for onerous tasks. In the Special Period, the very different requirement arose for him to choose officers for courses and postings in the business world and the economy, people who would be efficient and loyal and would not be improperly tempted by the glistening environment of international business to which many of them were to be sent.

Thus when he became president himself, he had a lifetime behind him of making difficult decisions on who should do what. This had created in the FAR an officer corps that some observers, including the excellent US analyst and close student of Cuban military affairs Frank Mora, have termed *Raúlista* with considerable exactness.[33] These officers are his picked men, and in some cases women, and owe their ascent to some major degree to him. They are, however, also highly competent and professional, and Raúl chose them for those qualities as well as their loyalty principally to the Revolution but also to him. They are in no way Raúlista as opposed to *Fidelista* and would be shocked to think that anyone saw them in that way. But they would usually be very proud to think of themselves as "Raúl's men."

It is likely that as in the forces, so in government, Raúl would wish to have *his* people around him. This is natural and he waited almost three years before he made it happen. There is nothing surprising about this, and reading too much into the sackings of March 2009 is ill-advised. However, it is apt to consider that he wanted to be surrounded by people who he knew to be competent and loyal and that would follow his lead, whether the decision on the path to take was one of more reform or less. Whichever way it led, it would be as a result of Raúl's decision. In the context of the politics of Cuba today, the decision to fire and replace seems only too logical, military in style, and, even more so, like all of Raúl's approaches to such decisions in the past.

Thus the naming of military officers to replace some of the civilians who left the cabinet should not be seen as a specifically militarizing influence. What is visible on the military front is the continuing improvement in the defense conditions of the country we saw in the years just before 2006 and Raúl's assumption of power. Recruitment into the regular force was obviously moving forward well, and the FAR was clearly able to recruit first-class students for the future officer corps, as well, despite the cuts it had suffered and the bottlenecks for promotion to which reference has been made and which had not by any means altogether disappeared.[34]

On the significant point of the conditions in military installations, it is important to note the great decay that had occurred in many of these, especially those units not doing mainline deterrence jobs of highest priority. Buildings were often in bad repair, housing shabby, furniture old and dilapidated, kitchens broken down and inefficient, and sports, cultural, and other recreational facilities in short supply; there existed often a scruffy atmosphere in general. Raúl had promised the FAR improvements in living conditions after so many years of shortages and not being a priority. While the crisis continued and in 2008 deepened yet again, in a great many installations real improvement occurred. This was especially true with regard to training conditions.[35] But some new barracks and recreational facilities have been coming on line as have new kitchens and furnishings in some places. And as we have seen, military pay has improved markedly, especially in the EJT. Things are distinctly looking up but have a long way to go to recover the high standards of the pre-1990 FAR.

Chapter 7

A Revolutionary Soldier and *His* Revolutionary Defense System

It remains for us to assess to what extent one can say that Raúl Castro is not only another type of officer from the Latin American norm, but also whether the degree of that difference from the mold can be considered to be "revolutionary," as suggested by the overall approach to this book. And in close connection to that question is the further one, as to what extent we can say that the forces and defense system he has been central, under Fidel, in setting up can be seen as not only different but revolutionary in comparison to fellow armed services elsewhere in the region. It is difficult indeed to divide the two questions, so overlap will be the rule here.

The Man and His Reflection of the Institution

If one is to summarize what we have already seen and add further light to the first question as to whether Raúl is of the Latin American mold, and if not, if that difference can be considered a drastic one, we can first speak of what we know so far. Let us first see how the traditional Latin American officer has tended to look.[1] In most of the region, and Cuba was no exception to this rule before 1959, the bulk of the officer corps has tended to come from lower-middle-class families and a very large percentage indeed from those of serving or retired senior NCOs.

Social mobility, always at a premium in the region, was in many countries most possible in the armed forces and access to officer rank was central to this. Senior NCOs usually observed this most acutely and thus wished for their sons to go to military college and become officers. In Latin America, essentially the only method to become an officer has been to pass through military college. There are rarely means to achieve officer status through promotion from the ranks or directly from university or secondary school. Thus entry into military college is the key. Indeed, in most countries one's results academically and militarily in that college will follow him throughout his career and have a significant impact on his promotions. Thus, cadets have very rarely come from the ranks of the traditional oligarchy and only on occasion from the upper-middle class because sons of families from those classes would rarely find the officer corps of the armed forces as appealing as other sectors to which they had ease of access. Traditional military families from the lower middle class tend to be massively represented in the officer cadet ranks of military colleges, reflecting their desire for the very difficult to obtain goal of social mobility.

The officer cadet then passes usually four or five years in a firmly military institution and becomes thoroughly acculturated to the military milieu and usually distanced from his civilian origins. His friends tend to be other cadets, his social life revolves around the college, and his studies and sports are deeply embedded in military life. While increasingly the current practice is that he obtains a degree with civilian value to it, he is nonetheless a distinct graduate of a military environment first and an academic one only secondarily.

Upon commissioning as an officer, the young man (or woman in recent times) is posted to a unit, but there the comparisons with most experience with modernized armed forces in the north end. For the Latin American officer can expect to spend a great deal more time on course than his counterpart from northern countries. He will go through junior staff college, a variety of promotions, specialty and refresher courses, staff college, and if promoted far enough, national war college or national defense college courses before reaching general or admiral rank. The amount of time away from troops and units, undergoing this formal training, is generally much greater than in the United States, British Commonwealth, or most NATO armed forces.

Thus, the Latin American officer is much more course-bound than these counterparts and is expected constantly to be attending very long professional courses and consequently be spending less time with his unit. The lack of direct experience of military conflict also affects this tendency to book learning as opposed to practical experience, a situation changing in many of the region's forces but which is still very much present today.

As a result, there are fewer occasions for Latin American officers to have active command of forces especially in the real test for the military, the area of active combat. Latin American forces other than Cuba's FAR in the last half century have only been involved in international combat in the Honduras-El Salvador war of 1969, the Falklands War of 1982, and the Ecuador-Peru conflict of 1995, although they have been mobilized often enough for crises, some of which have involved limited and desultory fighting, and have of course often been very much involved in domestic conflict and counterinsurgency and counterterrorism operations.

Thus senior officers can and do normally reach general rank without any combat experience whatsoever and with relatively little real operational time under their belts. This has of course changed with the expansion of peacekeeping duties especially after 1989. But peace-support roles in alliance with the United States, undertaken by three Central American armies in Iraq after the 2003 invasion, have been at company level and have not involved senior officers at all. And peacekeeping operations, outside of Haiti where Brazilian generals have had command from the beginning of the most recent operation, have rarely seen Latin American officers in the most senior positions. Given this and other traditions, senior rank is often a matter of seniority as much as any actually proven operational capacity.

Raúl could simply not have a more different career profile from senior officers who come from this more common Latin American experience. When he got his first command in preparation for the Granma landing, he had never been to a military college, although he had of course briefly attended a school with some military pretensions; he had to gain his rank through successful command in the field, in active wartime operations, against a regular army enemy.

Instead of having an infrastructure and traditions into which to fit himself, he had to build that infrastructure and lay the groundwork for a tradition. While he came from a reasonably well-to-do family, he had no military connections of any kind coming from that family environment and got to know military affairs through being dropped in at the deep end from the beginning, as one will recall from his experience of the abortive 1953 Moncada Barracks attack. While keen on military history, he did not have Fidel's breadth of knowledge in this area and had to rely on instinct to see him through.

A mere member of the ranks for Moncada, he had risen to junior officer rank through his work in prison, in training in Mexico, and in roles related to the departure of the expeditionaries for Cuba in the autumn of 1956. He was then an extraordinarily young man receiving tasks of enormous complexity in a rebel force with little practical knowledge of war. Within 15 months of the landing, however, as we have seen, he had his own quite independent force, which he had formed, organized, trained, educated, armed, and administered, and which he led to a series of victories against exceptional odds. And within ten more months, he had led that force to dramatic final success in his territorial area of responsibility.

When he became minister in 1959, he had no formal government experience, merely the organization and administration of his part of Oriente's Cuba Libre during the months of the Segundo Frente's operations as something like such a useful past. His rise from lieutenant to general de ejército and minister had taken only just over two years, which was not unknown, some would say, for the wild nature of much of Latin American politics, but certainly unusual in the context of a victorious rebellion against an established army. But that meteoric rise had occurred as a result also of proven skills and abilities that the Revolution needed and would need for some time. As mentioned elsewhere, given the threat the Revolution was facing, not to mention that to the very life of the comandante en jefe, it was inconceivable that the ministerial portfolio of defense and security would be given to anyone that Fidel did not think was both the best man for the job, and in this case the best meant also the most trusted.

In all of this, there was little enough of the routine military life common in Latin American armed forces. Training, education, advancement, and military life in the Ejército Rebelde could hardly have been any more different from that for an officer of a regular Latin American armed forces. Yet it would be wrong indeed to suggest it was not a military life. It most definitely was just that with combat—the supreme test of a military man—a fact of life. And the taking of hard decisions, the essence of an officer's career, was the daily reality of the young Raúl.

In addition, Raúl saw himself as a revolutionary leader not only using nontraditional means to wrest victory from a superior enemy, but also proposing as part and parcel of the way to victory the embodying of a revolutionary program and revolutionary virtues, as well as the implanting of a revolutionary society in territories controlled by him and his forces. His aim, shared with and inspired by his brother, was the remaking of Cuban society from top to bottom. And if in this, his goals seemed close to communist goals, Raúl certainly did not use conventional communist methods which were then calling for cooperation with other progressive forces to slowly build the objective conditions for revolution that all communists hoped at some distant time in the future to see.

Like Fidel, Raúl clearly had no intention to wait for those conditions to prevail but rather intended to act decisively to create them. Under his brother or on his own, he so acted and in or out of office remained the most determined of proponents of a powerful thrust toward communist goals. It must, however, be admitted that again like his brother, these goals, and the methods used to reach them, could often easily be seen as following a Cuban tradition, more closely based on the thoughts of José Martí than those of Marx, Lenin, or Stalin.

As has been said before, one does not want to go too far in suggesting that there is only one mold from which a Latin American officer could come. But there is a dominant one. Raúl does not come from this dominant mold. He is not like the bulk of Latin American officers in attitudes or experience. Like other revolutionaries of his era, his conclusion, from looking at his national and regional experience, was that only revolution, and not evolution, could solve the central issues of his country's independence and continue the drive for greater equality. He believed in radical change for his country and the adoption of radical methods to achieve its effective defense.

A Military Personality?

This book makes no attempt to be a biography of Raúl. However, no picture of his contribution to military life in Cuba could be even nearly complete without addressing the debate about his personality which affects his impact on the FAR as well as on Cuba more widely. The author is not a psychologist nor is he a great believer in the attempts of some historians to use psychological approaches to explain the actions of great personalities on the political stage. And even if he were, he would not, lacking knowledge in that field, be in a position to use such approaches.

The need is there, however, to at least consider those elements of Raúl's personality that impinge on our military story. There are certainly at least two main schools of thought on this, and on its effect on his military life. Roughly speaking, there is on the one hand an overwhelmingly dominant view on the island that Raúl is an officer of high personal and professional qualities, a man of honor, courage, and great sensitivity, a family man, and a man who has proven himself to be more than able to lead and organize armed forces.

On the other hand, there is a view dominant in the United States, and particularly within the exiled Cuban-American community in that country, that Raúl is a ruthless, scheming, uncaring, even cruel man, determined to assist his brother in the maintenance of a corrupt and vicious totalitarian system that holds its citizens in an island prison from which he ensures they can rarely escape. Brian Latell—a careful analyst of Cuba and especially of Raúl, but one who has not been able to engage with many Cubans outside the special conditions of defectors in the United States—probably sums up best, and not in such an exaggerated way, this latter view in his *After Fidel: The Inside Story of Castro's Regime and Cuba's Next Leader.*[2] He and many exiled Cuban-Americans point to issues mentioned before such as, among many others, Raúl's views on the need for severity in what they see as the "kangaroo trials" of 1959 and the 1960s, his work generally in setting up and running the security apparatus of a "totalitarian" state, his opposition to *glasnost* and *perestroika* in the Soviet Union, and more generally, his suppression of the academic *apertura* (opening up) on the island in the already-mentioned CEA affair of the mid-1990s, and of what they view as his slowness to reform since 2006.

After consulting the work of journalists and historians who have done nearly one hundred formal interviews with those officers who know Raúl best on the island, and after hundreds of more informal conversations with Cubans and foreigners from all walks of life who have known Raúl, this author must, with only the slightest nuance, come to the conclusion that the dominant view in Cuba appears to be much closer to the truth, as those readers patient enough to have come this far in reading this book will surely have surmised.

Let us look at some assessments of civilians and military officers who have known this man for many years and worked closely with him, always with an understanding that at least the officers in this situation are unlikely to criticize very severely their commander and minister in a public venue. We know that Celia Sánchez Manduley, confidante and probably the woman closest to Fidel until her death from cancer in 1980, and a woman of great discernment by all accounts, developed a close friendship with Raúl. Reports abound as to his pleasure at meeting her for the first time and of the depth of mutual respect and affection that they retained for one another over the years, right to the end. This was cemented in part by their work on military history, where Raúl was frustrated with the lack of academic work done on the study of the revolutionary struggle and Celia was given charge of the archive of the Revolution.[3]

We have also one of the first assessments of Raúl in print, that by Hilda Gadea, the Peruvian wife of Che Guevara, who met Raúl in

Mexico in 1955 when he was 24 years old. Referring to him as a close friend, she said, "He was merry, open, sure of himself, very clear in his exposition of ideas, with an incredible capacity for analysis and synthesis. This is why he got along so well with Ernesto."[4] It is worth noting that while that friendship may not have been as perfect as Che's with Fidel, it stood the test of time, and Che certainly did not suffer fools gladly or choose for his friends people who were not up to his very high moral and intellectual standards.

Closer to today, the then Major-General Leopoldo Cintra Frias, a man not known for holding back on his opinions, used in an interview during the worst stages of the Special Period, the adjectives *simple*, *sincero*, *humano*, *muy claro*, *realista*, and *preciso* (sincere, human, very clear, realistic, and precise) to describe his minister, insisting on the ease with which one could talk to him on any sort of problem, even the most serious and even the most personal.[5] His colleague, Major-General Néstor López Cuba, refers to Raúl's great interest in the troops and his constant and exhausting visits to field units, conversations with individual soldiers, and special combination of demanding approaches to instruction with a sincere desire to see personnel welfare of a high order.[6] The author's conversations with hundreds of junior servicemen confirm this view.

López Cuba is troubled by US views saying, "The image they have of Raúl is of an insensitive, authoritarian person. Unfortunately they know little of his virtues: his simplicity, his humanism, his concern for mankind, for his subordinates, for his family, for the people." He also insists on Raúl's great sense of humor to which he says so many in the FAR and in the general public constantly refer. He tells for example the story of how when the Russians during the Special Period hoped to sell some more Mig-29s to the Cubans to supplement the few the FAR already had, Raúl asked them how much they would cost. When the Russians told him they were $20 million each, he replied, "We'll sell you the six we have."[7] Major-General Enrique Carreras agrees with the need to be concerned about US attempts to particularly denigrate Raúl but feels they engage in this because they know very well just how impressive a man he is and "with him there will be no problems if something were to happen to Fidel."[8] This statement from the early nineties was prophetic indeed.

Outside the military field, assessments range widely but overwhelmingly speak of a man of great sensitivity, a great sense of the value of family life and friendship, and who sees himself as working for the betterment of mankind. Sometimes, as with his ability to win the sincere love of his beloved Vilma Espín, Cuban observers wax romantic. Referring to Vilma's time in the Sierra with Raúl in the Segundo Frente, Vilma's only biographer, Carolina Aguilar Ayerra, writes, "There too arose that love she had so hoped for. Vilma believed in love and knew how to wait to find it. There was born a pair of beings who have grown together, building their lives, parents of a family, an example of love and of the raising of their children and grandchildren."[9] She even goes so far as to compare the couple with perhaps the most famous love story of Cuban history, that between the superb cavalry commander of the first revolution against Spain, Major-General Ignacio Agramonte, and his adored Amalia Simoni.[10] Fidel's recent biographer, Claudia Furiati, likewise comes to the conclusion that behind the face of a man who is after all a military officer responsible for the defense of a besieged revolution is an organized and experienced commander but one that is not in any way *tan duro como aparenta* (as hard as he appears).[11]

General José Ramón Fernandez, as we have seen, agrees with this view and reinforces it with an assessment of Raúl's special role as the real force behind the magnificent Cuban program to bring literacy to so much of the Third World, called *Si, se puede* (Yes, you can, or yes, one can).[12] And General Villegas, already quoted, feels that if Raúl were in any way the type of man painted by most US sources, he would not have encouraged the writing of the oft-quoted series of dozens of interviews with Cuban generals undertaken by Luis Báez nor given those officers what was apparently carte blanche to say essentially whatever they wanted in those interviews.[13]

None of this can be conclusive. One does not expect that any of these observers would be in any case excessively critical of Raúl. But to suggest that they, those closest to the people who were or are themselves closest to Raúl, are all lying and simply saying what is expected, does not do credit to the quality of people they are and have been shown to be. We have also seen how the extensive research done by Tad Szulc, in what so many independent observers consider to be still the best and most balanced biography of Fidel, led to the same conclusions about the nature of his brother Raúl. In addition, this assessment agrees with that of the vast majority of persons with whom the author has conversed on this subject: businessmen foreign and Cuban, academics and especially economists who have worked closely and recently with him, foreign military officers and diplomats who do not depend in any way on Raúl's favor, and serving and ex-serving soldiers, sailors, and airmen who have had occasion to know him during their former careers in the ranks and who had no fear that their identity would be disclosed.

The Institution Itself

What of the institution itself? Has, and if so, how has this revolutionary leader, with the inspiration, direction and help of his brother, brought about armed forces that respond to this un–Latin American model and indeed can be seen as themselves revolutionary, as their very name suggests? To answer this question, we must ask again what that Latin American model tends to look like, recognizing once more that such a single model does not exist and that one is working here with general attributes usually but not always seen in the armed forces of the region.

It is generally held that Latin American armed forces are characterized by, among other things, certain habits of thought, ways of doing things, structures, weapons, links to the outside world, professional attributes, and the like which transcend the borders between their nations and arise from similar historical experiences and social and political realities. Domestic and international conflict, fractured civil societies, a powerful aspiration for democracy almost always frustrated by practical experience, and oligarchies of ferocious appetites and less than total devotion to a national idea, and thus a generally illegitimate dominant class and system of government; this has all led to armed forces reflecting various combinations of these conditions.

There can be little wonder that these military institutions reflect the negative elements of those societies as well as the positive. But it must be said that with such weak civil institutions, including the political parties and the middle class, government has tended to be corrupt, inefficient, and oriented around personalities or even potential *saviours*. Crises of legitimacy and leadership thus tend to be endemic. It would have been extraordinary if the armed forces, as the holders of state coercive power, had not grown to have great power. In most countries of the region, they have achieved enormous influence and have repeatedly and directly taken over the reins of government since independence two centuries ago. Only recently has this context shown great change but change of still uncertain duration.

Their sense of order, nearly ubiquitous status throughout the national territory, hierarchical system, command structure accepted by all as proper, discipline, habit of planning, flexibility, mobility, fitness, system of training and keeping up to date with their profession, and vast range of capabilities within their own structures already make them unique in their societies. But when these attributes are added to their status as *armed* and *available* at any time to governments with security problems of an often vital kind, the importance of the military becomes staggering and its centrality to the state and society more than manifest.

This state of affairs,[14] when added to the experience actually lived by these forces even before but especially since independence, must give them some specific features, listed below, which, while not present in all cases and requiring at times nuance, do tend to apply:

- a tendency to exaggerated numbers of senior officers for the size of the institution
- politicization through links with elements of the political process usually but not always on the right
- a tendency to institutional deliberation on national issues
- divisions between officers and other ranks along lines of race
- greatest power to the army but serious interservice rivalry
- "Prussianism"
- exaggerated sense of self-worth as the institutional embodiment of the highest of national values
- deprecatory attitude to politicians and the democratic process
- roles more linked to internal security than external defense
- little international combat experience
- small numbers of high-prestige weapons but most less modern
- armed forces as the "school of the nation"
- reliance on the United States for training, weapons, and equipment and doctrine
- corruption at high level when in government
- phenomenon of *acato pero no cumplo* (I respect but do not comply—that is, with the order received)
- excessive number of courses and insufficient time in real command
- excessive distance in the interaction between officers and other ranks, and privileges of officers unlinked to responsibilities for troops

Do the Cuban armed forces reflect these conditions, which are regarded as widespread or even nearly ubiquitous in Latin America's military institutions? In the area of an exaggerated number of senior officers relative to the size of the forces as a whole, there is some relation to the Cuban case but not one based on the same factors. In most of Latin America, the number of senior officers has in one way or another come down from Iberian practice and has been a fact of military life since independence at least. The status of general has been much sought after, and it has proven wise for politicians to ensure that there are plenty of such positions around for aspiring young officers and even for powerful landlords or other elements of the upper classes. It must also be said that the situation in regard to the excessively high number of senior officers serving has improved in recent decades.

In Cuba the number of senior officers is related to two factors, both of which have a considerable degree of legitimacy in military terms. A FAR with just over fifty-five thousand troops but with a requirement to mobilize many times that number when crises loom cannot expect to train senior officers for such a mobilization once it occurs. They must be available at once, and the only way that can be ensured is by having them in the ranks of the regular force, being trained and gaining further experience in their chosen career. The second factor is that the FAR still retains in the uniformed ranks many senior officers of the *histórico* (historic) type from the revolutionary struggle against Batista. They tend to have other more junior officers doing the practical jobs associated with the postings they currently hold, but it is felt that they give inspiration and a sense of history to the forces and the idea of national defense as a whole. Thus while Cuba certainly has more generals in uniform than would be normally warranted by the mere size of its regular forces, there are very good military reasons for this being the case.

On the issue of politicized armed forces, the FAR would proudly plead guilty but would do so in ways far from the Latin American norm.[15] It is not politicized in the sense of backing a particular political group within the day-to-day politics of the nation, but rather in that it is the embodiment of the defense of the revolutionary project of the island and of its government with a specific series of political goals in mind in terms of the transformation of the island into what it views as a better society. Its title of revolutionary is taken very seriously indeed; the FAR does not feel that any other would apply.

It does not, however, feel that it is institutionally available for the political objectives of one or other group within the body politic. Instead the FAR is only there for those objectives of national and revolutionary defense that the state has set upon it. Likewise the FAR would most definitely see itself as serving a national project of the left. Linked to this is the question of institutional deliberation on issues faced by the nation. The FAR is a disciplined military force that answers to the directives of the president. The FAR does not deliberate on national issues although officers of course have views on them. Orders are issued and obeyed along the highly disciplined lines Fidel and Raúl laid out in Mexico and have applied since then.

In the FAR, the officer corps is not divided from the mass of the soldiery by race. If it is true that there are fewer very senior officers who are black or mulato than their percentage in society as a whole, this is not in any way as obvious in the ranks of more junior officers. Black or mulato generals or admirals are rare, but among colonels and below such personnel are not. And the FAR recognizes the problem and seeks to address it with policies toward recruitment in the Camilito pre-military academy schools. As a matter of course, white soldiers serve under black officers and vice versa. There is room for improvement here, but the issue is not considered central or reflective of institutional racism or the like but rather of Cuban national reality over history. The FAR does, however, often have members who fear the general trend toward a return to open racism that many feel is now a fact of Cuban society today. Personnel expressing racist views in the forces, however, can expect short shrift from their seniors if such views are made in a public forum.

On the question of army dominance over the other two services, Cuba currently does appear to follow the Latin American norm. Until the Revolution, it did so in the usual manner, and indeed, despite a tiny air element, the Ejército Rebelde was a land force and had no navy or air force in the usual sense. What then happened was that in response to the nature of the US threat, and with the availability of equipment and weapon systems from the Soviet Union, the FAR built a limited blue-water navy capable of interception duties against any invasion force; the air force built a significant fighter, fighter-bomber, and reconnaissance capability for air and antilanding defense operations.

For those years, the army yielded up part but hardly all of its traditional superiority. However, as of today the nature of the blows the FAR received in the Special Period, and the more sophisticated nature of the two other services, meant that the navy and air force have taken most of the weight of reduction in defense capacities, and the army has recovered the bulk of its historic leadership. This needs nuance, however, since the three services are closely integrated in the FAR and there is in no way the interservice rivalry, especially on budget issues that one sees in most other national armed services, prevails on the island.[16]

"Prussianism," often characterized as excessive attention to military minutiae and those elements viewed as typical of the great discipline of the old army of Prussia, is very present in many Latin American armies especially those, such as Chile and Argentina, trained in the past by German military missions. The Cubans, like most Caribbean peoples, are not particularly given to such discipline or attention to military detail, and even the old army probably could be considered to have been relatively free of it. Certainly the FAR and the Ejército Rebelde had been spared it, although discipline could be tough, as we have seen.

The Soviet Armed Forces were, however, not only heirs to a czarist tradition of considerable aping of Prussianism, but also were highly respectful of what they viewed as the successes such an approach had given their German enemies. And they brought these views and practices with them in their guidance of the FAR during the 1960s, 1970s, and 1980s. But if the USSR was successful in implanting its ideas in the FAR in doctrine, equipment, weaponry, uniforms, procedures, administration, strategy and tactics, and the like, it most certainly was not able to implement Prussianism and the FAR remains a bulwark of *Cubanía* even with its exceptional discipline.

The FAR is a proud institution with a sense of its embodiment of national values and revolutionary ethics. But in no sense does it share with so many of their Latin American counterparts a feeling of the exclusiveness of its role in the first of these. The FAR feels that it shares with the state and people this context and in no way argues that it should somehow be considered different because it is the armed forces. For the FAR, Fidel's ideas are the continuation of those of José Martí and the other fathers of independence, and the revolutionary state and society that Fidel has brought into play is itself the embodiment of national values, and most definitely not only the forces that serve as that state and society's armed fist.

Before the Revolution, there is no doubt that the Cuban armed forces felt a deprecatory attitude toward politicians and democracy. And while the *politiquería* (vulgar political scheming) of those days is certainly looked down upon by the FAR today, national politics and those who engage in them in today's socialist state do not come in for such criticism. But Cuban politics are of course not those of a capitalist democracy along the Western model. Indeed, there is precious little democratic politics to be seen in Cuba if one is looking for a reflection of what is seen in Western Europe or North America. But if politics is seen as the play of forces over which Fidel and Raúl sit and includes the political process of the Cuban state today, there is little criticism in the FAR of them, although there is much individual comment among members of the military forces about the economy and the like.

As for roles more linked to domestic requirements than foreign, the FAR is a true exception to the Latin American norm. As seen throughout this paper, the FAR takes as an article of faith that el ejército no tira contra el pueblo and does not train for internal security roles. It is of course true that in the 1960s, in the face of largely but not exclusively foreign-inspired bandidismo, the FAR conducted major operations at home. It is also true that antidrug and anti-illegal migration duties have an internal component. But in the Latin American context of internal security, the FAR can be considered a clear exception to the rule of a central role in this control. The Cuban state has other security forces for such roles as these and believes it can afford to spare its armed forces from this task, considering that things would have to go very badly indeed in terms of domestic disorder before they were called in.[17]

It has been shown that under Raúl the FAR has had long and extensive experience abroad completely beyond anything imagined by any other Latin American military at any time in its history. The internationalist missions in Africa, the Middle East, and Latin America have brought the institution unparalleled combat and foreign experience unknown elsewhere in the region; Brazilian World War II initiatives, a tiny effort by Mexico in that same war, small-scale Colombian action in Korea, and even the disastrous Argentine involvement in the Falklands War are all rather far away in time and actual impact on the way their forces do things.[18] This is not in any sense the case in Cuba, where the FAR has relatively recent and relevant experience to draw on. This is changing to some extent with other countries' involvement in peacekeeping and peace support operations abroad, but most of these so far have seen little actual fighting.

The acquisition and holding of arms is also different to a degree from the experience of most Latin American forces. In Cuba, the context is not one of small numbers of sophisticated weapons, deployed with great éclat, combined with a large number of older types, as elsewhere.[19] Rather the weapons situation is one where essentially all of them are now old even if in their time they were highly sophisticated, and this is true even of those being used by units that are vital elements of the deterrence system. Those units will doubtless have ones that are in better repair and kept up to standard so that they can be used if needed, but they will not have new and up-to-date ones because there has been no way of purchasing new systems since 1990.

The army as the "school of the nation" is a principle of many armed forces using the continental model of organization that all socialist countries also adopted but which began its life essentially with the French Revolution. In most countries of Latin America, it has been based on compulsory military service with, among other objectives, that of making the recruit, from wherever in the nation he comes and from whatever social and ethnic background, an effective and loyal citizen. This often includes as much work making him literate as it does making him a good soldier.

The FAR is no stranger to this idea or this tradition. But it sees itself as only *part* of this system, furthering it but hardly its main element. The good national educational system that the Revolution has produced is, in Cuba, the school of the nation, not, in this other sense, the armed forces. They take recruits who are already literate and entirely "Cubanized" and make them good soldiers, and that is their job. The experience of military service, it is hoped, will make them even better citizens; it will also include political education and the honing of skills developed initially in the family and at school, but that is not its raison d'être. Obligatory military service is about national defense in a much more strictly military sense although also in that wider sense of service to the Revolution and the patria.

On the question of military connections with, and the influence of, the United States, the FAR is as different as it could possibly be from the rest of Latin America. If the armed forces of Cuba before 1959 reflected the highest levels of penetration by US military influences in Latin America—a distinction probably shared by the Dominican Republic, El Salvador, Haiti, Honduras, Nicaragua of the time, and Venezuela—since the Revolution that relationship has been completely left behind. The Sovietization of the 1960s and 1970s ensured that this was the case as did the determination of Cuban military leadership to end that connection. The departure of remaining US military personnel in January 1961 with the rupture of diplomatic relations was merely the most visible of the steps taken. Most Latin American countries, even most of those in the Bolivarean reformist camp, still maintain close military relations with the United States, but this is in no sense the case in Cuba.

On corruption when in government, the pattern in Cuba is once again far from the Latin American normal experience of immense personal and state corruption when the institution is actually in power. The FAR has problems of corruption, as discussed, but they in no way compare with the usual historic experience of the armed forces of Central America, the Andean countries, Argentina, or Brazil, or those of the smaller countries of the region when they have had direct control of the reins of the state. There corruption has tended to be not only endemic but has also benefited from almost total impunity, as well. This is in no sense the situation in Cuba, where in any case it is difficult to speak of the FAR as "in power" in any institutional way of a Latin American kind.

Equally, acato pero no cumplo is not a problem one sees in the FAR. Personnel of the armed forces generally obey as good military men and women and orders are complied with as a matter of course. The strong traditions of discipline inculcated in the Ejército Rebelde as long ago as its original members' training in Mexico are still the rule. Indeed, as is obvious, it is not really possible to speak of a professional military functioning in a modern sense where such a phrase can apply.[20]

The relationship of officers to other ranks is also very different in the FAR from that seen in most Latin American armed forces. While officers have privileges, these are directly related to their command responsibilities and their need to have more time than other ranks for the administration and running of their formations, units, and subunits. FAR officers are visibly shocked when they hear of phenomena such as officers having different rations from other ranks, being served meals first and the troops afterward, or having access to vastly better conditions of service than the personnel serving under them—that is, being in every sense of the word in a different social class (and often of a different race) from them, all elements which are commonplace in the armed forces of most of the region.

Thus almost across the board, we can see armed forces that are very different indeed from what is generally considered the Latin American norm. Again, one must insist that there are 20 Latin Americas, as Marcel Niedergang reminds us in his seminal work, and that the differences between armed forces such as the Chilean and the Honduran are simply massive.[21] But we can join all students of those forces in saying that some features of their institutions are either shared by all or a great many of them. The FAR diverges from these norms to a vast degree in almost every sphere.

This is the work of Fidel and of Raúl who, as we have seen, have chosen another approach to the organization of their armed forces, making them truly the armed fist of the Cuban Revolution and in so doing making them revolutionary in both the political and organizational sense. If they are proud of their traditions, even those that have on occasion rather oddly been grafted onto the forces by Sovietization, they do not in general approach problems from a traditionalist perspective at all. In fact, of course, they could not do so even if they wished to. The enormous range of roles into which they have been thrust over the half-century of the Revolution, and the variety of conditions they have faced in the different moments of that period, have ensured that tradition *must* be a good servant and not a bad master, to return to a previous point. The FAR rarely has had, and currently does not have, the luxury of getting it wrong.

Chapter 8

Conclusions

This book has been about the military man and commander Raúl Castro Ruz and the armed forces in whose formation and management over nearly half a century he has had such a massive role. It has not sought to be a biography of this figure but rather to highlight the kind of commander he was, the impact his way of approaching his role had on the functioning of those armed forces, and the way those armed forces reacted to his command. It has also been possible to argue that he has taken into political power and his search for answers to the very serious challenges Cuba and its revolution face elements of a military style of government that have become also characteristic of his way of doing business and getting the results he wishes.

It is the conclusion of this study that Raúl Castro is indeed an "other" type of military leader compared to the kind most Latin American military establishments and training systems have tended to produce, and that he can well be properly ranked with the tradition of progressive general officers such as Praats and Schneider in Chile, Caamaño in the Dominican Republic, Árbenz in Guatemala, Perón in Argentina, Velasco Alvarado in Peru, and others.[1] Indeed, perhaps he could be considered the epitome of the type in that he is not just non-traditional but rather revolutionary in the full sense of the word.

Raúl Castro has during his whole lifetime been a revolutionary. His thinking about the government Cuba needed, the changes the island required, and, for the purposes of this study, the type of armed forces without which the Revolution would inevitably fail has tended to be revolutionary. He did not just wish to see change. He wished to see a transformation of government, society, and armed forces on the island. Following the lead and command of his elder brother, whether one approves or not, he has dedicated his life to effecting these changes.

In order to do so, the creation of a viable revolutionary force to overthrow the previous government and to prepare the way for the installation of a new one with a revolutionary program was a sine qua non for success. That force, once successful, found itself obliged not only to defend the Revolution against enmity abroad and at home from very powerful forces indeed, but to do so while it also contributed across the board in national reorganization and regeneration.

For nearly half a century, Raúl supported Fidel as a loyal subordinate in the construction of the needed defensive apparatus, and in the creation of the context in which it would take on its many roles and adapt its basic strategy to changing times. For several years now, he has even had to step in and take on the overall conduct of the effort to ensure the Revolution's recovery and survival after the vast challenges of the Special Period.

Raúl is at the time of writing approaching his eighty-first year with great vigor and determination to carry on the struggle and ensure success as in the past. But part of that determination is linked to the idea of institutionalizing the Revolution in ways that will permit its survival after the departure of its historic figures, including himself. If he is successful, history may judge that effort to have been by far his greatest contribution of all.

Be that as it may, this study has hoped to show that in this man, and in the forces he, under Fidel, has created and led, is very much found the less well-known tradition of Latin American commanders who do not accept a given and historic link with the oligarchies of their countries. Nor do they believe that military forces are inherently conservative and anti-progressive, and do not accept that dominance by the United States is the unavoidable fate of the region's countries or armed forces. Finally, they do not believe the military establishments they lead are destined to be used more often against their people than against their peoples' enemies abroad.

The authors of the series for which this book was originally prepared were asked to discuss in the Latin American context, *otros soldados,*

> soldiers whose actions have had a different character to that assigned habitually to men of arms and military institutions...involved in political process that have taken place outside the economic establishment and/or the situation of the dominating elites...have achieved the modification of a current reality, (and) have provided

a rearticulating of the links between armed forces and society or political system.[2]

Raúl is an "otro" in that sense. There is no doubt that he has had to make very difficult decisions on immensely serious issues where, in his view, the survival of all he believed in was at stake, and that some of those decisions led to unfortunate consequences in terms of human rights and other ethical matters. But Cuba is not a country in a normal situation where it is easy to judge the rights and wrongs of the case. It is in a very real sense under siege by the most powerful nation in the history of the world, 150 kilometers away as we said at the beginning of this study, by law and policy determined to destroy the social, economic, and political system of the country. This is unique. And the responses to the threat it poses have had to be unique, as well.

If Fidel has shown the greatest ingenuity in designing those original responses, it has often been to his younger brother that he has turned in order to ensure that those responses functioned and especially that they could be sustained in the face of the threats involved. This task has required a man and a national defense system and armed forces that represent that *otredad* (otherness) and that capacity to think in highly original ways about how to proceed. Raúl has proven he is that man. And he has been crucial in helping found and configure another kind of armed forces to do the job.

It remains to be seen whether he can carry on the success he has had with the armed forces and national strategy for defense and deterrence into the even more taxing conditions of national government as a whole in the Cuba of today and of the near future. It is clear that reform is in the air and that it is going to be faster than most observers believed, but it seems certain as well that such change is to be firmly in the hands of the current leadership or those they choose to succeed them, if Raúl has anything to do with it.

The challenges are simply massive: a largely disaffected urban youth, corruption at endemic levels, vested interests in the Party and elsewhere wishing to see the reforms fail, bureaucratic inertia at often astounding levels, bloated state institutions as well as labor arrangements, a poor and unsustainable work ethic which Raúl has been keen to remove after so many years of sway—these are some of the many social and economic issues seemingly without end that the country faces. And on the international level, one sees a context by no means entirely favorable to independently minded leftist governments almost entirely without access to credit or even especially helpful partners.

ALBA is clearly much better than nothing, but Cuba's problems of a small and vulnerable economy, closely linked to international trading conditions, cannot be solved by membership in such a bloc alone. Cuba is far from isolated diplomatically, but it is not able so far to turn that opening, to any state or bloc, into real and permanent solutions to its problems.

In this daunting context, however, Raúl can doubtless look to some elements of light and comfort. Chief among these must surely be the armed forces that he has had such a key role in establishing and leading. With their flexibility and proven loyalty, he can at least plan for a future with more hope and above all more security than would otherwise have been possible. Cuba needs both.

Notes

Avant Propos

1. Ernesto López, *El primer Perón: el militar antes que el político*, Buenos Aires, Capital Intelectual, 2009, p.11.

1   Youth, Soldier, Officer, First Command

1. On Raúl's early life see many sources such as Tad Szulc, *Fidel: a Critical Portrait* (New York: Avon Books, 1986); Claudia Furiati, *Fidel Castro: la historia me absolverá*, (Mexico: Plaza Janés, 2003); and Ignacio Ramonet, *Cien Horas con Fidel* (Havana: Oficina de Publicaciones del Consejo de Estado, 2003). As mentioned, alas, there is nothing like a proper biography of Raúl and this book is certainly no attempt to provide one.
2. There is still debate as to the timing, context, and meaning of his joining the communist movement and many serious scholars question the degree to which it is possible to refer to him as a Marxist or communist as of these very early days when he was only 21.
3. Szulc, *Fidel*, 358–359.
4. "Now we really will win the war." Raúl Castro, "Diario de campaña," in *La Conquista de la esperanza: diarios de campaña de Ernesto Che Guevara y Raúl Castro Ruz 2 de diciembre de 1956–19 de febrero de 1957* (Havana: Editorial Verde Olivo, 2005), 120.
5. There is still debate, into which Fidel has entered himself, as to exactly how many men assembled at that time and how many rejoined the group later on. But all sources agree that the figure was certainly more than 10 and fewer than 20.
6. For the story of those struggles, see Louis Perez, *Cuba between Empires, 1878–1902* (Pittsburgh: University of Pittsburgh Press, 1982).
7. Olivia Diago Izquierdo, *Epopeya de la Libertad* (Havana: Verde Olivo, 2007), 27–31.
8. "Gee, brother, I feel like a child who has left his father's arms and started to walk on his own." Ibid., 39.

9. In his zone of operations there were over 2,600 soldiers of Batista's army with many more soon sent there on news of the arrival of Raúl's party. See Mayra Aladro Cardoso et al., *La Guerra de Liberación Nacional en Cuba 1956–1959* (Havana: Casa Editora Abril, 2007), 116–118.

10. Roberto Pérez Rivero, *La Guerra de Liberación Nacional* (Santiago de Cuba: Editorial Oriente, 2006), 62–63.

11. Aladro Cardoso et al., *La Guerra*, 157–160.

12. Cited in Rolando Marrón, *Fuerza Aérea Rebelde Segundo Frente Oriental "Frank País"* (Havana: Editorial Ciencias Sociales, 1988), 34.

13. Szulc, *Fidel*, 448–50.

14. For the extraordinary history of this tiny force, see Marrón, *Fuerza Aérea Rebelde*, especially 159–173.

15. Izquierdo, *Epopeya de la Libertad*,86–87; and Jose Suárez Amador, *Maestros de verde olivo*, (Havana, Ciencias Sociales, 2009), 2-20.

16. Aladro Cardoso et al., *La Guerra*, 53–54.

17. Marrón, *Fuerza Aérea Rebelde*, 126.

18. For example, see Enrique Acevedo, *Descamisado* (Havana: Editorial Capitán San Luis, 2002), 151.

19. Izquierdo, *Epopeya de la Libertad*, 114–116.

2 Minister but Still a Soldier

1. Tad Szulc, *Fidel: a Critical Portrait*, (New York: Avon, 1986), 479–484; Thomas G. Paterson, *Contesting Castro: The United States and the Triumph of the Cuban Revolution* (New York: Oxford University Press, 1994); and Morris H. Morley, *Imperial State and Revolution: The United States and Cuba, 1952–1986* (Cambridge: Cambridge University Press, 2002). This refers to the bearded state of many of the rebels who had fought in the mountains and in the harsh plains campaigns of the invasion. *Barbudos* means "bearded ones" in Spanish.

2. For Raúl's own thoughts on this, see his speech "El VI Aniversario del Ejército Juvenil del Trabajo y la Inauguración de la Escuela Vocacional Militar 'Camilo Cienfuegos,'" in *Raúl Castro: Selección de discursos y artículos 1959–1974* (vol. I) (Havana: Editora Política, 1988), 77–79.

3. See Luis M. Buch Rodríguez, *Gobierno Revolucionario cubano: génesis y primeros pasos* (Havana, Editorial Ciencias Sociales, 1999), especially 31–32.

4. For this fascinating story, see Francisco Pérez Guzmán, *La Habana: clave de un imperio* (Havana: Ciencias Sociales, 1993).

5. Francisco Castillo Meléndez, *La Defensa de la isla de Cuba en la segunda mitad del siglo XVII* (Sevilla: Padura, 1996). See also

Roberto Antonio Hernández Suárez, *Ejército colonial en Cuba, 1561–1725* (Havana: Verde Olivo, 2011), 19–34.

6. See throughout Gustavo Placer Cervera, *Ejército y milicias en la Cuba colonial (1763–1783)* (Havana: Agencia Española de Cooperación Internacional para el Desarrollo, 2009).

7. US investors had taken advantage of the bankruptcy of virtually all the island's aristocracy caused by the war to produce total dominance of the country's economy. For the best study of the Cuban military in these years, see Marilú Uralde Cancio, "La Guardia Rural: un instrumento de la dominación colonial," in *La sociedad cubana en los albores de la República*, ed. Mildred de la Torre (Havana: Editorial Ciencias Sociales, 2002), 255–282. For 1902–1959, see Rafael Fermoselle, *The Evolution of the Cuban Military 1492–1986* (Miami: Ediciones Universal, 1987), and José M. Hernández, *Cuba and the United States: Intervention and Militarism, 1868–1933* (Austin: University of Texas Press, 1997), 109–115. See also Oliver Cepero Echemendía et al., *Historia militar de Cuba*, (Havana: Verde Olivo, 2011), 71–98.

8. Servando Valdés Sánchez, *Cuba y Estados Unidos: relaciones militares 1933–1958* (Havana: Editora Política, 2005), 63–92, especially 89.

9. "The passion for money and violence." This quote, and much of the support for this analysis, comes from Sánchez, *La Elite Militar en Cuba (1952–1958)* (Havana: Editorial Ciencias Sociales, 2008).

10. For an excellent look at what military values are supposed to be, and how they have been perverted in much of the region, see Prudencio García, *El Drama de la autonomía militar* (Madrid: Alianza, 1995).

11. Enrique Acevedo, *Descamisado*, (Havana: Editorial Capitán San Luis, 2002), especially 243 and 283. See also Szulc, *Fidel*, 483. For Fidel's own views and his admission that the handling of the trials was an error, see Ignacio Ramonet,*Cien horas con Fidel*, (Havana: Consejo de Estado, 2003), 250–253.

12. See the interesting comparisons between Fidel and Che on these matters in the first chapters of Paul Dosal, *Comandante Che: Guerrilla Soldier, Commander and Strategist, 1956–1967* (University Park, Pennsylvania State University Press, 2003).

13. Szulc, *Fidel*, 113–114, 124, and 308. See also Fidel's own comments in Ramonet, *Cien Horas con Fidel*, 157,

14. See Luis M. Buch Rodríguez and Reinaldo Suárez Suárez, *Otros pasos del gobierno revolucionario cubano* (Havana, Ciencias Sociales, 2002), 219–223.

15. Ibid., 90–93.

16. The base for expansion was exceptionally small. The size of the Ejército Rebelde of the time is a subject of debate to this day. Fidel is surely accurate when he says that it was never larger than three thousand personnel. See Ramonet, *Cien horas*, 231–232. See also Neil

Macaulay, "The Cuban Rebel Army: a Numerical Study," *Hispanic American Historical Review* (May 1978): 284–295.

17. Rodríguez and Suárez Suárez, *Otros pasos*, 100–109, and Szulc, *Fidel*, 505–506.

18. Raúl had married in January, as soon as his duties allowed it, his beloved Vilma Espín, the legendary urban organizer of the 26 de Julio, then his inseparable companion in the Sierra Cristal, and soon to be a major feminine stimulus of reform in the government. She was especially keen on a militia that would give women ways to express their determination to defend their own achievements of the Revolution. See Carolina Aguilar Ayerra, *Por siempre, Vilma* (Havana: Editorial de la Mujer, 2008), especially 36, 41.

19. See Juan Carlos Rodríguez, *Girón: la batalla inevitable* (Havana: Editorial Capitán San Luis, 2005), 86.

20. For a detailed look at the history of the militias and reserve forces of revolutionary Cuba from their inception to today, see Hugo Rueda Jomarrón, *Tradiciones combativas de un pueblo: las milicias cubanas* (Havana: Editora Politica, 2009).

21. See many personal accounts of those days in Luis Báez, *Secretos de generales* (Barcelona: Lozada, 1997).

22. María del Pilar Díaz Castañón, *Ideología y revolución: Cuba, 1959–1962* (Havana: Ciencias Sociales), 118–119.

23. For the role of women in the fighting, see Mary Alice Waters, *Marianas in Combat: Teté Puebla and the Mariana Grajales Platoon in Cuba's Revolutionary War 1956–58* (New York: Pathfinder, 2003).

24. See Hugh Thomas, *Cuba: The Pursuit of Freedom* (London: Eyre and Spottiswoode, 1971), 1237–1244.

25. For the most complete work so far on the Soviet-Cuban military connection, see Yuri Pavlov, *The Soviet-Cuban Alliance 1959–1991* (New Brunswick, NJ: Transaction Publishers, 1993).

26. For the whole period see the interview with General Néstor López Cuba, in Báez, *Secretos de generales*, 7; and Suárez Amador, *Maestros*, 233 For the early years, see Raúl's view in his September 30, 1966, speech, "La Graduación de Estudiantes Integrantes de la Marcha del Segundo Frente 'Frank País,'" in Raúl Castro, *Discursos*, 176

27. For the story of Raúl's desire to be a bullfighter, see Otto Hernández Garcini et al., *Huellas del exilio: Fidel en México 1955–1956* (La Habana: Casa Editora Abril, 2007), 73–74, 147.

28. Interview with General Enrique Carreras in Waters, *Haciendo historia: entrevistas con cuatro generales de las Fuerzas Armadas Revolucionarias de Cuba* (Havana: Editora Política, 2006), 51.

29. Interview with General José Ramón Fernández, ibid., 80

30. Raúl Castro, Speech of September 11, 1959, "La Amenaza de la Revolución cubana," in Raúl Castro, *Selección de discursos*, 7–9.

31. Szulc, *Fidel*, 491–492.
32. José Abreu Cardet, *Cuba y las expediciones de junio de 1959* (Santo Domingo: Editora Manatí, 2002), especially 30–60.
33. Miguel Zaballa Martínez, *La Artillería en Cuba en el siglo XX* (Havana: Ediciones Verde Olivo, 2000), 60–65.
34. Szulc, *Fidel*, 544.
35. By far the best and most complete handling of this invasion is found in Peter Kornbluh, ed., *Bay of Pigs Declassified: The Secret CIA Report of the Invasion of Cuba* (New York: New Press, 1998).
36. For the Cuban side of the story, see throughout Rodríguez, *Girón*, especially 169–170.
37. Szulc, *Fidel*, 545.
38. Rodríguez, *Girón*, 296.
39. Zaballa Martínez, *La Artillería en Cuba*, 81.
40. Tomás Díez Acosta, *Octubre 1962: a un paso del holocausto* (Havana: Editora Política, 2008), 46–47.
41. Ramonet, *Cien horas*, 307–311.
42. Claudia Furiati, *Fidel Castro: la historia me absolverá*, (Barcelona: Plaza Janés, 2003), 421–422.
43. For Fidel's strategic calculations here, see Manuel E. Yepe, "La postura cubana ante la invasión soviética a Checoslovaquia en 1968: un reexamen crítico," *Temas*, no. 55 (July–September 2008), 82–90.
44. One of the few works on this fighting is José R. Herrera Medina, *Operación Jaula: contragolpe en el Escambray* (Havana: Editora Verde Olivo, 2006).
45. For the full story, see Pedro Etcheverry Vázquez and Santiago Gutiérrez Oceguera, *Bandidismo: derrota de la CIA en Cuba* (Havana: Editorial Capitán San Luis, 2008).
46. Josep Colomer, "Los militares 'duros' y la transición en Cuba," *Encuentros de la cultura cubana*, XXVI/XXVII (fall/winter 2002–2003), 148–167.
47. These figures are taken from International Institute for Strategic Studies, *The Military Balance*, London, for the years in question.
48. Interview with Brigadier-General Harry Villegas in Waters, *Haciendo Historia*, 102.
49. Szulc, *Fidel*, 524.
50. The official order to unseat Fidel came only in March 1960, but President Eisenhower admitted, "*En cuestión de semanas, después que Castro entrara en La Habana, nosotros, en el gobierno, comenzamos a examinar las medidas que podían ser efectivas para reprimir a Castro*" (In a matter of weeks, after Castro entered Havana, we in the government began to examine measures that could be effective in repressing Castro). The Spanish quote is from Dwight D. Eisenhower, *Los Años de la Casa Blanca* (New York: Doubleday, 1966), 404, quoted in Rodríguez, *Girón*, 25. As elsewhere, the translation is the author's.

51. María Teresa Malmierca, *Comités de Defensa de la Revolución: aporte de la Revolución cubana* (Havana: Ediciones Extramuros, 2005), 24–25.
52. Ibid., 36–37.
53. Ibid., 47, 81. See also Jorge Lezcano Pérez, "La Defensa de la Revolución por las masas" in *Memorias de la Revolución*, II, ed. Enrique Oltuski Ozacki et al. (Havana: Editora Imagen Contemporánea, 2008), 132–140, especially 137.
54. For context, see ", Los militares 'duros,'" 150–152.
55. In Spanish, a major disturbance often is termed after the place where it takes place with the suffix "azo" added. This rioting, usually known in Cuba as the Maleconazo after the great seaside avenue on which it took place, came after two smaller incidents in earlier months but, related to frustrations over emigration, it was much more serious, affecting central Havana and involving thousands of people. Only the intervention of Fidel in person put an end to the incident. See several important references to this in Homero Campo and Orlando Pérez, *Cuba: los años duros* (Mexico City: Plaza y Janés, 1997).
56. The subject here is Raúl as military man so, as mentioned, little discussion here is given to these institutions. For more on them, see the author's chapter "Cuba," in *Handbook of Global Security and Intelligence*, vol. II, ed. Stuart Farson et al. (New York: Praeger, 2008).
57. See also Leon Goure, "Soviet-Cuban Military Relations," in *The Cuban Military under Castro*, ed. Jaime Suchlicki (Miami: University of Miami, 1989), especially 183–184.
58. See the English version of Brian Latell's book, *After Fidel: The Inside Story of Castro's Regime and Cuba's New Leader* (New York: Palgrave/Macmillan, 2006), 102. Pascoe Pierce left memoirs of his stay in Cuba in *En el filo: historia de una crisis diplomática, Cuba 2001–2002* (Mexico City: Ediciones Sin Nombre, 2004).
59. For the official story of MININT and Seguridad del Estado, see Cuba, Ministerio del Interior, *Las Reglas del juego: 30 años de la seguridad del estado*, 2 vol. (Havana: Editorial Capitán San Luis, 1992).
60. Thomas, *Cuba*, 372–373.
61. Zaballa Martínez, *La Artillería en Cuba*, 110.
62. The official relationship was not always smooth. Even the ferocious critic of Castro, Brigadier-General Rafael del Pino, the FAR's most senior defector, has said Cuban-Soviet military relations were "indifferent and at times antagonistic. They [the Soviets] do not have the slightest influence on the decisions Cubans make." Quoted in Jay Mallin, *History of the Cuban Armed Forces: from Colony to Castro* (Reston, VI: Ancient Mariners Press, 2000), 333.
63. Conversations with several retired senior Cuban officers in Havana, Cienfuegos, and Camaguey over the period 1998 through 2000.

64. Francisco Forteza, "Cuba: Ejército productivo," World Data Service, WDS-015, August 5, 2003.
65. Raúl Castro, "Discurso del V Aniversario de la Columna Juvenil del Centenario y la Constitución del Ejército Juvenil de Trabajo," Camagüey, August 3, 1973, in *Discursos y Artículos*, 245–259. An *arroba* is traditionally given as being 25 pounds in weight, although in more recent times in Spain it is considered to be 15 kilograms.
66. Comisión de Historia del Ejército Oriental, *Reseña histórica Ejército Oriental: Señor Ejército!* (Santiago: Editorial Oriente, 2008), 30.
67. For the most complete work on this subject, see Piero Gleijeses, *Misiones en conflicto: La Habana, Washington y África 1959–1976* (La Habana: Editora Ciencias Sociales, 2002). For the FAR there, see Raúl Menéndez Tomassevich, *Patria africana* (Havana: Editora Ciencias Sociales, 2006). For a frank recent view, see Enrique Acevedo, *Fronteras* (Havana: Editorial Abril, 2010).
68. The Brazilian effort is described in Celso Castro, *A invenção do Exército brasileiro* (Rio de Janeiro: Zahar, 2002), Catherine Prost, *L'armée brésilienne, organisation et rôle géopolitique de 1500 à nos jours* (Paris: L'Harmattan, 2003), and Ricardo Bonalume and César Campiani Maximiano, *Onde estão os nossos héróis?* (Sao Paulo: Santuario, 1995).
69. Zaballa Martínez, *La Artillería en Cuba*, 139–152.
70. For a pictorial and textual idea of this, see Cuba, Ministerio de las Fuerzas Armadas Revolucionarias, *Fuerzas armadas revolucionarias de la República de Cuba* (Havana: Editorial Orbe, 1976).

3 More Thinking Required: The 1980s and the Weakening of the Soviet Connection

1. For the relationship with COMECON and its members, see Julio A. Diaz Vázquez, "Cuba y el CAME," *Temas*, no. 55 (July–September 2008): 115–124.
2. See Wayne Smith, *The Closest of Enemies* (New York, Norton, 1987).
3. Claudia Furiati, *Fidel Castro: la historia me absolverá*, (Mexico City, Barcelona: Plaza y Janes, 2003), 538.
4. General Vo Nguyen Giap, *Guerra del Pueblo; ejército del pueblo* (Havana: Ciencias Sociales, 2008).
5. See, for example, the interview with General José Ramón Fernández in Mary Alice Waters, *Haciendo historia: entrevistas con cuatro generales de las Fuerzas Armadas Revolucionarias de Cuba*, (New York: Pathfinder, 2001), 71–72.
6. Raúl Castro, speech entitled "La Constitución de un batallón masculino y una compaña femenina de las Milicias de Tropas Territoriales (MTT)," Santiago, January 21, 1981, from Raúl Castro, *Selección de discursos y artículos* II, 169–180.

7. Maria Teresa Malmierca, *Comités de Defensa de la Revolución: aporte de la Revolución cubana*, (Havana: Extramuros, 2005), 91.
8. Interview with General Néstor López in Waters, *Haciendo historia*, 17.
9. Raúl Castro, "XXX Aniversario del Desembarco del Granma," *La Revista Militar*, December 2, 1986: 288–291.
10. Miguel Zaballa Martínez, *La Artillería en Cuba en el siglo XX*, (Havana: Verde Olivo, 2000), 115.
11. See Domingo Amuchástegui, "Las FAR: del poder absoluto al control de las reformas," *Encuentro de la cultura cubana*, XVI/XXVII (autumn/winter 2002–2003): 133–147, especially 134–135, and Brian Latell, "The Military in Cuba's Transition" (unpublished paper, Georgetown, 2002), 14.
12. For a view of the wider impact over time on the Cuban economy, see Rafael Alhama Belamaric et al., *Perfeccionamiento empresarial: realidades y retos* (Havana: Ciencias Sociales, 2001).
13. See for example Furiati, *Fidel Castro*, 554.
14. Armando Ferrer Castro, *Conexión en Cuba: la historia de la poderosa red de funcionarios cubanos con el narcotráfico internacional* (Mexico: Planeta, 1990).
15. For this story, see Francisco Arias Fernández, *Cuba contra el narcotráfico: de víctimas a centinelas* (Havana: Editora Política, 2001), 64–85.
16. For Fidel's view of the Ochoa Affair, see Ignacio Ramonet, *Cien horas con Fidel* (Havana: Consejo de Estado, 2003), 419–435.
17. Furiati, *Fidel Castro*, 549–551. President Reagan had himself said in 1983, "There is strong evidence that Castro officials are involved in the drug trade, peddling drugs like criminals, profiting on the misery of the addicted." See Jay Mallin, *History of the Cuban Armed Forces: From Colony to Castro*, (Reston, VI: Ancient Mariners Press, 2000), 350.
18. Interview with General José Ramón Fernández, in Waters, *Haciendo historia*, 81. Raúl's views are in his later interview, "Somos los más antidroga del mundo," *El Sol de México*, April 23, 1991: 20.
19. Quoted in Raúl Marín, *¿La hora de Cuba?* (Madrid: Editorial Revolución, 1991), 10.

4   The Special Period for Raúl, the FAR, and Cuba

1. These and other figures come from the excellent account of these years in Homero Campo and Orlando Pérez, *Cuba: los años duros*, (Mexico City: Plaza y Janés, 1997), especially 14–15.
2. Interview with General José Ramón Fernández in Mary Alice Waters, *Haciendo historia: entrevistas con cuatro generales de las Fuerzas Armadas Revolucionarias de Cuba*, (New York: Pathfinder, 2001), 90.
3. Raúl Castro, interview "Somos los más anti-drogas del mundo," *El Sol de México*, April 23, 1991, , and A. B. Montes, "The Military

Response to Cuba's Economic Crisis" (Washington, DC: Defense Intelligence Agency, 1993), 21, and interview with Brigadier-General Orlando Almaguel Vidal in Luis Báez, *Secretos de generales* (Barcelona: Losada, 1997), 246.

4. Fidel Castro, *Un grano de maíz: conversación con Tomas Borge* (Havana: Oficina de Publicaciones del Consejo de Estado, 1992), 148.

5. Rafael Hernández, "El Hemisferio y Cuba: una postdata crepuscular a la cumbre de las Américas," *Cuadernos de Nuestra América*, XII, no. 24 (July–December 1995): 71–80, and Cuba, Oficina Nacional de Estadística, *Anuario Estadístico de Cuba 1990–1992*.

6. See Miguel Zaballa Martínez, *La Artllería en Cuba en el siglo XX* (Havana: Verde Olivo, 2000), 117, 155–156.

7. Interview with General Enrique Carreras, in Waters, *Haciendo historia*, 55–56.

8. This author is able to elaborate on some of these US-related issues, and on US positive reactions to Cuba's efforts, in his *Cuba's Military 1990–2005: Revolutionary Soldiers in Counter-Revolutionary Times* (New York: Palgrave/Macmillan, 2005), especially 103–147.

9. Interview with Major-General Néstor López Cuba in Waters, *Haciendo Historia*, 57.

10. Raúl Castro, "Somos los más antidroga del mundo," *El Sol de México*.

11. International Institute for Strategic Studies, *The Military Balance 2001–2002* (London, 2002).

12. For one exposition of this view, see Antoni Kapcia, "Political Change in Cuba: Before and After the Exodus" (occasional paper no. 9, University of London Institute of Latin American Studies, London, 1995).

13. See Cesar Gómez Chacón, "Una prueba de confianza," *Granma*, April 4, 1991, 3

14. Cuba, Oficina Nacional de Estadística, *Anuario Estadístico de Cuba 1996*.

15. For General Rosales del Toro's own views on these subjects, see his interview in Báez, *Secretos*, 574.

16. This officer became minister of the FAR after Raúl assumed the presidency.

17. Interview with former head of the UIM General Luís Pérez Róspide, in Báez, *Secretos*, 547.

18. Interview with General Néstor López Cuba in Waters, *Haciendo historia*, 31.

19. The story of the system, and of Raúl's role in setting it up, is told in Miguel Angel Puig Gonzalez et al., *Fortalezas frente a huracanes (1959–2008)* (Havana: Editorial Cientifico-técnica, 2010).

20. For points relevant to this, see the remarks of Major-General Samuel Rodiles Planas in "Operación Cabaiguán marcha satisfactoriamente," *Granma*, June 27, 2007, 4.

21. This comment is the result of dozens of conversations with retired, serving, and militia officers, senior NCOs and other ranks over the years of the Special Period.
22. Interview General Néstor López Cuba, in Waters, *Hacienda Historia*, 30.
23. Interview with General Harry Villegas, ibid., 111.
24. See interview with General Enrique Carreras, ibid., 53.
25. Interview with General José Ramón Fernández, ibid., 80–81.
26. See José Hernández, "Contra la corrupción," *Tribuna de La Habana*, May 25, 2003, 3.
27. See for comparisons with the FAR on this Arnoldo Brenes and Kevin Casas, *Soldados como empresarios: los negocios de los militares en Centroamérica* (San José: Fundación Arias, 1998).
28. Interview with Major-General Enrique Carreras in Báez, *Secretos*, 79.
29. Interviews with Generals López Cuba and Villegas in Waters, *Haciendo historia,*, 7, 109–110.
30. Interview with Vice-Admiral Pedro Pérez Betancourt, in Báez, *Secretos*, 139–140.
31. Quoted from interview in Waters, *Haciendo historia,*, 29–31.
32. Quoted from interview, ibid., 53, 114–115.
33. Interview with General Juan Escalona Reguera, head of civil defense in Báez, *Secretos*, 508.
34. See Sergio Díaz-Briquets and Jorge Pérez-López, *Corruption in Cuba: Castro and Beyond* (Austin: University of Austin Press, 2006) for the very good theoretical discussion on corruption therein.

5 Partial Recovery and Last Years as Minister

1. See interesting themes in this regard in Joseph Tulchin et al., *Cambios en la sociedad cubana en los noventa* (Washington, DC: Woodrow Wilson International Centre for Scholars, 2005), especially Viviana Togores González, "Ingresos monetarios de la población, cambios en la distribución y efectos sobre el nivel de vida," 187–210. Also useful is Omar Everleny Pérez Villanueva et al., *Cuba: reflexiones sobre su economía* (Havana: Prensa de la Universidad de La Habana, 2002).
2. These figures come from the appropriate annual volumes of Cuba, Oficina Nacional de Estadística, *Anuario Estadístico de Cuba*, 1990 and beyond. See for some helpful thoughts on how to study these, Omar Everleny Pérez Villanueva, "La Administración del presupuesto del estado cubano: una valoración," in *Centro de Estudios de la Economía Cubana, La Economía cubana en el 2001* (Havana: CEEC, 2002), 19–40.
3. Joaquin Roy, *Cuba, the United States and the Helms-Burton Doctrine: International Reactions* (Gaineseville: University of Florida Press, 2000).

4. See Lars Schoultz, *National Security and United States Policy towards Latin America* (Princeton: Princeton University Press, 1987).
5. Christopher Marquis, "Report Downplaying Cuban Threat Back to Review," *The Miami Herald*, April 8, 1998. See also his "Pentagon Want U.S. Military to Work with Cuba," *The Miami Herald*, February 21, 1998.
6. See throughout Horacio Veneroni, *Los Estados Unidos y las Fuerzas Armadas de América Latina* (Buenos Aires: Periferia, 1973).
7. See Morris H. Morley and Chris McGillion, *Unfinished Business: America and Cuba after the Cold War, 1989–2001* (Cambridge: Cambridge University Press, 2002), 36, and Richard Gott, *In the Shadow of the Liberator* (London: Verso, 2000), 25.
8. Carmelo Mesa-Lago, *Are Economic Reforms Propelling Cuba to the Market?* (Miami: North-South Center Press, 1994), 7.
9. In the early years of the Sino-Soviet conflict, Cuba had tried a connection with both countries. Soon, however, it was clear to Raúl and Fidel that Moscow offered vastly more to the island than did Beijing. See Tad Szulc, *Fidel: a Critical Portrait* (New York: Avon, 1986), 510–511. Only in the mid-1980s, when Soviet assistance became less certain, did Havana open a defense attaché office in Beijing and begin to study the potential for much cooperation.

6 A Military Man as President

1. Fidel Castro Ruz, *Sobre temas militares* (Havana: Imprenta General de las FAR, 1990).
2. Ramonet, 702–704 and Tad Szulc, *Fidel: a Critical Portrait* (New York: Avon, 1986), 643–644.
3. Conversations with NATO security specialists in Cuba, August–September 2006.
4. The author witnessed this personally on the streets of the Vedado neighborhood of Havana on the morning of August 1, 2006.
5. See Carlos Alzugaray Treto's important and influential "Cuba cincuenta años después: continuidad y cambio político," *Temas*, LXI, 2010, 37–47, especially 42.
6. Conversations with both the Canadian and Spanish defense attachés at the time. Cubans often use humor to express the realities of current situations, and one of the main jokes going about the country at the time was that if one asked a young Cuban what he or she would do first if suddenly made president of Cuba, the reply would unhesitatingly be "I'd resign."
7. These points are based on widespread but informal conversations with Cuban officials, economists, and academics over the period August 2006 and January 2007.
8. Szulc, *Fidel*, 65.

9. For an exceptional and wide-ranging view of Fidel's style of government, including the massive positive side but insisting also on questions of his often inhuman pace of doing business, frequent impatience with underlings, occasional impulsiveness in decisions, perfectionist approaches, and tendency to vanity, see throughout ibid.
10. Raúl Castro, "¡Y a trabajar duro!", *Granma*, December 29, 2007.
11. This is the conclusion reached by all the economists and political scientists the author spoke with during the period 2006 through 2008.
12. *Pensamiento Propio* was a journal of Marxist thought but had included articles critical of Soviet Marxism. See Dick Cluster and Rafael Hernández, *The History of Havana* (New York: Palgrave/Macmillan, 2008), 240. The "affair" was when Raúl acted firmly to end what he saw as excessive linkages being made between the prestigious Centro de Estudios de las Americas and foreign academic institutions and think tanks working on Cuba and Latin America. For a critical look at these events and Raúl's role in them, see Maurizio Giuliano, *El Caso CEA: intelectuales e inquisidores en Cuba* (Miami: Ediciones Universal, 1998). For the Mexican case, see Szulc, *Fidel*, 358–359. See more on Raúl's role in this affair in Claudia Furiati, *Fidel Castro: la historia me absolverá* (Barcelona: Plaza Janés, 2003), 594.
13. Speech of Raúl Castro, *Granma*, July 27, 2007.
14. This reflected his views as expressed to economists working closely with the FAR at least as early as a year before his taking over the government. This assertion comes from conversations with a number of economists doing studies for him during that time and in the first years of his government.
15. See Norma Vasallo Barrueta, "El Género: un análisis de la 'naturalización,'" in *Heterogeneidad social en la Cuba actual*, ed. Luis Iñiguez Rojas and Omar Everleny Pérez Villanueva (Havana: Imprenta de la Universidad de Havana, 2004), 91–104.
16. Raúl said on the debates, "*Todos serán escuchados con atención, coincidan o no con la opinión de la mayoría. No aspiramos a la unanimidad, que suele resultar ficticia, en este o en cualquier otro tema.*" (All will be listened to with attention, whether they coincide with majority opinion or not. We do not aspire to unanimity which tends to end up being fictional, in this or any other theme.). This is change indeed in how the Cuban government does things. See Raúl Castro, "Trabajar con sentido crítico, creador, sin anquilosamientos ni esquematismos," quoted in Alzugaray, "Cuba cincuenta años después," 44.
17. See throughout ibid.
18. This section is largely the result of the intelligent and careful work of Mark Frank, Reuters correspondent in Havana, especially his "Raúl Castro's Road to Reform," Reuters, September 20, 2010.

19. See the unequalled reporting of Marc Frank, especially his reports entitled "Raul Castro's Road to Reform in Cuba," Reuters, July 2, 2009, September 19, 2009 and April 13, 2011, IDmN132238894 and IDmN14256472.
20. Alzugaray, "Cuba cincuenta años después," 40.
21. See for example R. Evan Ellis, *China-Latin America Military Engagement: Good Will, Good Business, and Strategic Position*, (Washington, Strategic Studies Institute, 2011), especially 9-10.
22. "Destacan cumplimiento de acuerdos Rusia y Cuba," *Granma*, January 26, 2010, 4. Still Russia was honored at the 2010 Havana Book Fair, and its presence was notable, including the visit of the foreign minister. See "Sostiene Raúl encuentro con el Canciller de Rusia," *Juventud Rebelde*, February 13, 2010.
23. For recent trends, see Miguel Manrique, *Cambio y restructuración del ministerio de la defensa y la fuerza armada venezolana a comienzos del siglo XXI* (paper for ADEFAL, Madrid, 2006), 8, and for the longer view, see the Venezuelan chapter in Adrian J. English, *The Armed Forces of Latin America* (London: Jane's, 1984).
24. See José Toro Hardy, "El Nuevo Metrópoli," *El Universal* (Caracas), May 30, 2003, 1–2. For the general picture diplomatically and politically, see Carlos Romero, "Cuba y Venezuela: la génesis y el desarrollo de una utopía bilateral," in Luis Fernando Ayerbe (ed.), *Cuba,Estados Unidos y América Latina frente a los desafíos hemisféricos* (Barcelona: Icaria, 2011), 159-202.
25. "Entrega Reino Unido Donativo a Cuba," *Granma Internacional*, February 21, 1999, 9. The United States is essentially the only country active regionally in the anti-drug field that does not have a full anti-drug cooperation agreement with Cuba. The island has such accords with 12 Latin American, 6 Commonwealth Caribbean, 6 European, and 2 other countries. For details, see Francisco Arias Fernández, *Cuba contra el narcotráfico: de víctimas a centinelas* (Havana: Política, 2001), 171–172.
26. It is of interest that such naval ship visits of good will have not only involved the British and French. Other NATO nations have also paid such visits, with the Spanish doing so on several occasions. In addition, other allies of the United States in Latin America have done the same.
27. Juan Francisco Arias Fernández, *Drogas y mentiras: dos agresiones contra Cuba* (Havana: Editorial Capitán San Luis, 2008), 72–75.
28. See, for example, United States, US State Department, *International Narcotics Control Strategy Report*, Washington, DC, 2005.
29. This author is able to elaborate on these points in his "Confidence Building and the Cuba-United States Confrontation" (international security research paper, Department of Foreign Affairs and International Trade, Ottawa, , March, 2000).

30. Raúl issued the invitation again at the February 2010 Playa del Carmen meeting to found a Latin American and Caribbean organization aimed at effective political coordination in the region. See *Juventud Rebelde*, February 24, 2010, 4.
31. Alzugaray, "Cuba cincuenta años después," 45.
32. Antoine Henri de Jomini, *Précis de l'art de la guerre* (Paris: Flammarion, 1977).
33. See Frank Mora, "From Fidelismo to Raúlismo: Civilian Control of the Military in Cuba" (unpublished paper, September 2000), 6, and also his "Raúl Castro and the FAR: Potential Future Roles in a Post-Fidel Cuba" (unpublished paper, Memphis, 2001).
34. See "La Utilidad como condición," *Juventud rebelde*, June 27, 2007, 4.
35. See for example Lourdes Pérez Navarro, "Conducir, tirar y volar en realidad virtual," *Granma*, June 8, 2007, 7, and the very interesting article "Paisaje verde olivo renovado," *Juventud Rebelde*, January 18, 2011.

7 A Revolutionary Soldier and *His* Revolutionary Defense System

1. Much of the basis of this analysis is found in the extensive literature on this subject mentioned. See also Rut Diamint, ed., *Control civil y fuerzas armadas en las nuevas democracias latinoamericanas* (Buenos Aires: Grupo Editor Latinoamericano 1998), Frederick Nunn, *Yesterday's Soldiers: European Military Professionalism in South America 1890–1940* (Lincoln: University of Nebraska Press, 1992), Augusto Varas, *La Autonomía militar en América Latina* (Caracas: Nueva Sociedad, 1988), Brian Loveman and Thomas Davies, eds., *The Politics of anti-politics: the Military in Latin America* (Wilmington, DE: Scholarly Resources Books, 1997), and Edwin Lieuwen, *Arms and Politics in Latin America* (New York: Praeger, 1961).
2. Brian Latell, *After Fidel: The Inside Story of Castro's Regime and Cuba's Next Leader* (New York: Palgrave/Macmillan, 2006).
3. Pedro Álvarez Tabio, *Celia: ensayo para una biografía* (Havana: Consejo de Estado, 2004), 197–198, 247, 291.
4. Tad Szulc, *Fidel: a Critical Portrait* (New York: Avon, 1986), 335.
5. Interview with Major-General Leopoldo Cintra Frias, in Luis Báez, *Secretos de generales* (Barcelona: Losada, 1997), 491.
6. Interview with Major-General Néstor López Cuba, in Mary Alice Waters, *Haciendo historia: entrevistas con cuatro generales de las Fuerzas Armadas revolucionarias de Cuba* (New York: Pathfinder 2001), 22.
7. These quotes come from ibid., 23–25.

8. Interview with Major-General Enrique Carreras, ibid., 51.
9. See Carolina Aguilar Ayerra, *Por siempre, Vilma*, (Havana: Editorial de la Mujer, 2008), 143.
10. Ibid., 154. Also see, for a better understanding of the links between the experience of the two couples, the biography by Roberto Méndez Martínez and Ana María Pérez Pino, *Amalia Simoni: una vida oculta* (Havana: Ciencias Sociales, 2009).
11. Claudia Furiati, *Fidel Castro: la historia me absolverá* (Mexico City: Plaza y Janés, 2003),607.
12. Interview with Major-General José Ramón Fernández in Waters, *Haciendo historia*, 90.
13. Interview with Major-General Harry Villegas, ibid., 9.
14. The author does a more systematic assessment of this in his Hal Klepak, *Cuba's Military 1990-2005: Revolutionary Soldiers in Counter-Revolutionary Times* (New York: Palgrave/Macmillan, 2005), 214–238.
15. For example, see the interview with General Harry Villegas, in Waters, *Haciendo historia*, 111.
16. See throughout Francisco Rojas Aravena, ed., *Gasto militar en América Latina: procesos de decisiones y actores claves* (Santiago: FLACSO, 1994).
17. See Human Rights Watch, *Cuba's Repressive Machinery: Human Rights Forty Years after the Revolution* (New York: Human Rights Watch, 1999) for an overview of those institutions but one which pays little attention to Cuba's strategic context.
18. For Brazil, see Ricardo Neto Bonalume and Cesar Campiani Maximiano, *Onde estão os nossos heróis?* (Sao Paulo: Santuaro, 1995). For Mexico, see Marco Moya Palencia, *1942: Mexicanos al grito de guerra!* (México: Porrúa, 1992), 35–77. For Colombia in Korea, see its national chapter in Adrian English, *The Armed Forces of Latin America* (London: Jane's, 1984).
19. See throughout English, *The Armed Forces*.
20. Otto Hernández Garcini et al., *Huellas del exilio: Fidel en México, 1955-1956* (Havana: Editorial Abril, 2007), 147–159.
21. Marcel Niedergang, *Les Vingt Amériques latines* (Paris: Seuil, 1969).

8 Conclusions

1. In the context of that series of volumes, it is interesting to note that Fidel also has cited a list of "progressive commanders" that includes Guatemala's Jacobo Árbenz, the Dominican Republic's Francisco Alberto Caamaño, Mexico's Lázaro Cárdenas, Venezuela's Hugo Chávez, Argentina's Juan Domingo Perón, Brazil's Luis Carlos Prestes, Uruguay's Liber Seregni, Panama's Omar Torrijos, and Peru's Juan Velasco Alvarado. For Fidel's surprising attitude toward

what he considers a second, nonrightist tradition of military leaders in Latin America, see Ignacio Ramonet, *Cien horas con Fidel* (Havana: Consejo de Estado, 2007), 589–590.

2. Ernesto López, *El primer Perón: el militar antes que el político* (Buenos Aires: Le Monde Diplomatique/Capital Intelectual, 2008), 15.

Index